SQUIRE

C000212304

OF

CALKE ABBEY

Extracts from the journals of Sir George Crewe
of Calke Abbey, South Derbyshire, 1815-1834

Selected and edited
by
Colin Kitching

Scarthin Books of Cromford
Derbyshire
2004

THE EDITOR

Colin Kitching was educated at Sedbergh and Oxford, where he read modern history. During Royal Navy service in World War II he saw action in the Atlantic and Mediterranean, and took part in the Dieppe raid and the Normandy invasion. Post-war work experience was as a hospital administrator, followed by 26 years in charge of personnel and industrial relations for Pirelli Limited. He lives in the historic village of Repton, Derbyshire.

In retirement – encouraged by his wife, Betty, founder of the Repton Village History Group – Colin Kitching has revived his academic interests, with particular reference to local history. Researching, transcribing and editing these extracts from Sir Crewe's journals took eleven years to complete. He hopes to publish further material in due course.

Cover photograph of Calke Abbey by David Mitchell

Design: Guy Cooper

Phototypesetting: Techniset Typesetters, Newton-le-Willows, Merseyside

Printing:

Published by Scarthin Books, Cromford, Derbyshire, 1995

Reprinted 2004

ISBN 0 907758 84 3

Sir George Crewe with his eldest son, John.
Painted in 1828 by Ramsey Richard Reinagle.

FOREWORD

Early in the 1980s I was privileged to be the first historian to be given access to the archives of the Harpur-Crewe family at Calke Abbey in Derbyshire. The spectacle of seven hundred years of accumulated parchment and paper lying in disorder in the Muniment Room and elsewhere in that vast house was physically daunting but historically enticing. Out of the archival chaos there gradually emerged the story of a great estate whose owners for the last two hundred years had been remarkable for their reclusive habits: from Sir Henry Harpur, the 'isolated Baronet', in the reign of George III, to Charles Harpur-Crewe, whose death in 1981 at last broke the spell that had bound Calke for so long. To that pattern of aristocratic eccentricity there was one exception: Sir George Crewe, the owner of Calke from 1819 to 1844. As conscientious as his father had been self-centred, as public-spirited as his son and grandson were to be neglectful of their social obligations, Sir George Crewe was the first member of his family to take an active part in local and national life for half a century. For twenty-five years he managed his extensive estates with an exemplary combination of efficiency and Christian charity.

Throughout most of his life Sir George Crewe kept a journal which was at once a record of his daily life as landowner, magistrate and (later) MP, and at the same time a private confessional. For, like W.E. Gladstone, he felt the need to justify himself, 'not to posterity but to God'. To the modern reader these records of spiritual introspection are both tedious and embarrassing. But Sir George was also an acute observer of contemporary society at all levels. In the pages that follow, Mr. Kitching's judicious selection of passages gives a lively picture of life in Derbyshire in the early nineteenth century as seen through the eyes of an intelligent and compassionate man painfully aware of human short-comings. At Calke Abbey today the modern visitor can see the great house as an architectural monument that has been preserved almost unaltered since Sir George's time. In this book they can recapture some of the daily life of what was once both a fmily home and the hub of a great estate.

Howard Colvin
Fellow of St John's College,
Oxford

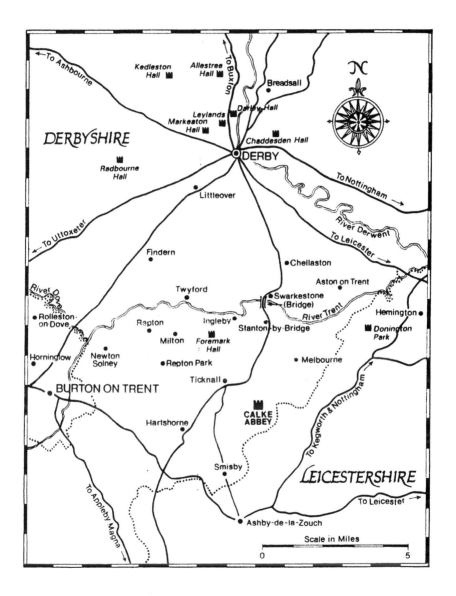

To Ashbourne
Kedleston Hall
Allestree Hall
To Buxton
Breadsall
Leylands
Markeaton Hall
Darley Hall
DERBYSHIRE
Chaddesden Hall
Radbourne Hall
DERBY
To Nottingham
Littleover
To Uttoxeter
River Derwent
To Leicester
Findern
Chellaston
Aston on Trent
Twyford
Swarkestone (Bridge)
River Dove
River Trent
Hemington
Rolleston-on-Dove
Repton
Ingleby
Stanton-by-Bridge
Donington Park
Milton
Foremark Hall
Horninglow
Newton Solney
Repton Park
Melbourne
BURTON ON TRENT
Ticknall
To Kegworth & Nottingham
Hartshorne
CALKE ABBEY
To Appleby Magna
Smisby
LEICESTERSHIRE
To Leicester
Ashby-de-la-Zouch

Scale in Miles
0   5

CONTENTS

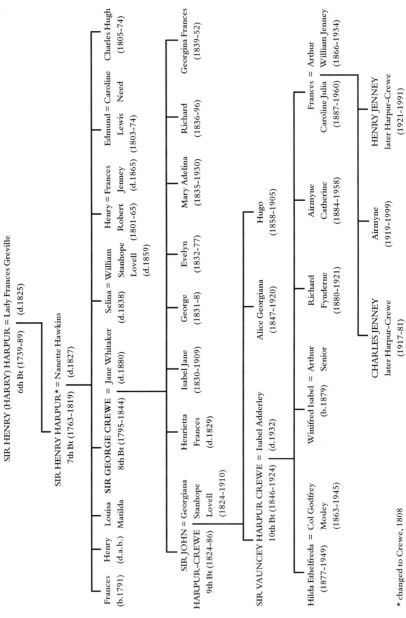

SIR HENRY (HARRY) HARPUR = Lady Frances Greville
6th Bt (1739-89)   (d.1825)

SIR HENRY HARPUR* = Nanette Hawkins
7th Bt (1763-1819)   (d.1827)

Frances   Henry   Louisa   SIR GEORGE CREWE = Jane Whitaker   Selina = William   Henry = Frances   Edmund = Caroline   Charles Hugh
(b.1791) (d.a.b.) Matilda   8th Bt (1795-1844)   (d.1880)   (d.1838)   Stanhope   Robert   Jenney   Lewis   Need   (1805-74)
                                                                        Lovell   (1801-65)   (d.1865)   (1803-74)
                                                                        (d.1859)

SIR JOHN = Georgiana   Henrietta   Isabel Jane   George   Evelyn   Mary Adelina   Richard   Georgina Frances
HARPUR–CREWE   Stanhope   Frances   (1830-1909)   (1831-8)   (1832-77)   (1835-1930)   (1836-96)   (1839-52)
9th Bt (1824-86)   Lovell   (d.1829)
                   (1824-1910)

                                       Alice Georgiana   Hugo
                                       (1847-1920)   (1858-1905)

SIR VAUNCEY HARPUR CREWE = Isabel Adderley
10th Bt (1846-1924)   (d.1932)

Hilda Ethelfreda = Col Godfrey   Winifred Isabel = Arthur   Richard   Airmyne   Frances = Arthur
(1877-1949)   Mosley   (b.1879)   Senior   Fynderne   Catherine   Caroline Julia   William Jenney
              (1863-1945)   (1880-1921)   (1884-1958)   (1887-1960)   (1866-1934)

                              CHARLES JENNEY   Airmyne   HENRY JENNEY
                              later Harpur-Crewe   (1919-1999)   later Harpur-Crewe
                              (1917-81)   (1921-1991)

* changed to Crewe, 1808

INTRODUCTION
CALKE ABBEY AND THE HARPUR-CREWE FAMILY

Hidden away near the village of Ticknall in rural South Derbyshire, Calke Abbey has been the stately home of the reclusive Harpur-Crewes for close on 300 years. Virtually unknown throughout this period, except locally, Calke became a cause célèbre in 1983. This arose from the disagreeable fact that, following the death of Charles Harpur-Crewe in 1981, a capital transfer tax bill of over £8 million had fallen due, with interest accumulating daily while it remained unpaid.

What was the new owner, Henry Harpur-Crewe, to do? The bleak answer was – sell the house, its contents and as much of the estate as would satisfy the tax demand. But the world of heritage conservation became aware of some remarkable features of the house – in particular that, because of the Harpur-Crewes' aversion to change, the contents of Calke Abbey constituted (to use the cliché which stuck) a time capsule. The weight of influential opinion in favour of preserving the house became irresistible. Finally, in his Budget of March 1984 the then Chancellor, Mr Nigel Lawson, allocated £4.5 million to the National Heritage Fund; this, together with substantial contributions from the National Trust, English Heritage and the Trustees of the Harpur-Crewe estate, brought about a happy ending. The National Trust acquired Calke Abbey on 1st March 1985, and set in motion a long and costly process of repairs and conservation. So it was not until Easter Saturday, 1989, that the house was opened to the public on a regular basis: the park, however, was made available to South Derbyshire's walkers and picnickers as early as the autumn of 1985.

So much for Calke Abbey: now for the Harpur-Crewes. The family's fascinating history is told in Howard Colvin's sumptuous book "Calke Abbey, Derbyshire: A Hidden House Revealed" (1985). Briefly, the story began in the mid-16th century when Richard Harpur, a successful lawyer, acquired property in South Derbyshire by virtue of his marriage to Jane Findern; she belonged to a family long connected with the village of Findern, between Derby and Burton-on-Trent. The property lay in and around such villages as Findern, Ticknall, Stanton-by-Bridge and Repton – and also at Swarkestone where Richard and Jane made their home.

Richard Harpur's son, John, inherited Swarkestone and the remainder of his father's lands in 1622. In the same year one of John's sons, Henry, bought a house and land at Calke. In 1679, following various lateral inheritances during the 17th century, Henry's grandson, Sir John Harpur, became heir to all the Harpur estates based on Swarkestone, Calke and Breadsall (north of Derby). In this way the seat of the senior Harpur moved from Swarkestone to Calke.

Sir John had suddenly become a very rich man – but did not enjoy his wealth for long, dying in 1681. His baby son and heir, also John, came of age in 1701 and in due course made an advantageous marriage with the youngest daughter of Lord Crewe, of Steane in Northamptonshire. From her the Harpur-Crewe designation eventually derived.

This Sir John made good use of his fortune. To mark his elevated position in society it was he who built the present house at Calke in the period 1701-03. Sir John died in 1741, to be succeeded by his son Henry. He, in turn, was followed by another Henry – usually known as Sir Harry. After his death in 1789 the heir was yet another Sir Henry – Sir George Crewe's father.

This Sir Henry was indeed an oddity. Inordinately shy, he shut himself up in his own world and took little part in public life. He scandalised his peers by taking a lady's maid as his mistress and then marrying her. She seems to have made him a good wife, however, quite apart from bearing seven children, of whom George was the third.

Sir Henry's interest in wild life, alive or dead, was a trait which reappeared in his descendants. More intellectual than most of his predecessors, he created the library in the house; he also carried out much landscaping work in the park.

Sir Henry's relationship with his heir, born in 1795, was formal and distant. For some inexplicable reason George was rarely permitted to be with the family at Calke once he had started his schooldays at Rugby. While he was a pupil there his holidays were spent in the kindly care of Lady Skipwith of Newbold Hall, some three miles from Rugby. George's harsh exile from home seems to have continued until his father's death in 1819. He was not allowed to go to Oxford or Cambridge after Rugby, but was despatched to a private tutor in Suffolk, a period the young man described thus in the 1821 diary:

"At this time, it being the wish of my dear Father that I should not go to College, he chose a situation for me with a Private Tutor, the Rev. Thomas

Allsop, (of) Fressingfield in Suffolk. This gentleman was of unusually austere, reserved disposition, and after having introduced me to two or three of the most respectable Families in the neighbourhood, shut himself up entirely. Not to this day has he ever seen company, excepting his Wife's Relations, and occasionally receiving the visits of very old and intimate College Friends".

All in all, what a curious upbringing for the heir to an immense estate! Moreover, Sir Henry kept his exiled son so short of money that, in spite of his natural frugality, George was often broke. On 11th August 1815 (aged 20) he wrote:

"I have just had an application for the payment of a small bill which brings with redoubled force to my mind the state in which I now am. I have one solitary coin in my purse, value 3 shillings, and a few half-pence. Beyond this I am not worth one farthing. My half-Guinea, which I had treasured up for so long a time, is gone . . . I am now in that situation that I am really quite ashamed to show my face, and what is more degrading I cannot but imagine that the people in the village have already observed it".

George's longing to go home for Christmas is conveyed by his diary entry for 2nd December 1815:

"I prayed to God that if it were His will I might have the inexpressible pleasure of visiting my dear Relations this Christmas. I mentioned it in my last letter to my Father, in answer to which he only says he thinks it would be better to defer my visit until the days get longer when he adds, (no stronger incitement to compliance could I wish for) I might be able to enjoy more of his company".

Bleak though George's existence was during this period, it seems to have produced one happy consequence. It must have been then that, among "two or three of the most respectable Families in the neighbourhood" to whom Mr Allsop introduced him, were the Whitakers, of Mendham, only a few miles from Fressingfield. George fell in love with the Rev. Thomas Whitaker's eldest daughter, Jane. Sir Henry (of course) adopted a dismissive attitude to the romance and sorely tested his son's powerful sense of filial duty.

What the outcome of the love affair woud have been if Sir Henry had lived longer is an intriguing speculation. His death in 1819, aged only 54, changed everything, however. The accident which caused it was described by George on 6th February 1822:

"This is the third anniversary of the melancholy accident which deprived me of a beloved parent. It is also, of course, the third anniversary of my being placed in the high and responsible situation of Life in which I now find myself

... Should any of my friends and relatives hereafter read these hasty lines I will record that my poor Father was one of the most awful instances of sudden death I ever heard of. On this day three years back, he was at Acklow House, Edgware Road. He took an early dinner and set off, about four o'clock, to drive his Phaeton to Barham House (in Hertfordshire) ... He drove safely until he came within two hundred yards or three from Barham House gate when he appeared, on a sudden, to drive furiously and, no doubt without seeing where he was going altho it was quite daylight, drove against a small post on the left hand side of the road and was in an instant precipitated to the ground – at which instant no doubt but that the fatal blow was struck and Life, in an instant, extinct".

So at the age of 24 a frustrated young man unexpectedly became Sir George Crewe, Baronet, the owner of a stately home, Calke Abbey, and master of thousands of acres of land in Derbyshire and Staffordshire. Overwhelmed though he was by a highly developed sense of responsibility for his employees and tenants, George nevertheless relished the new-found freedom to decide things for himself: by September he had married Jane Whitaker, who proved to be a most suitable partner.

To their dismay, however, five years passed before a child – John – arrived. But he was then followed by the birth of seven more children (three boys and four girls), of whom two died young. Mary Adeline, who was born in 1835, lived until 1930. Lady Crewe herself died in 1880.

Like his father, Sir George disliked life outside his own domain. A shy man whose health was never robust, he nevertheless undertook public duties because he felt he had to, in return for his privileged position. It was not in his nature to make a name for himself in these activities: but whether as a magistrate, High Sheriff of Derbyshire or a Member of Parliament his actions were governed always by moral principles and never by expediency.

The character of the man stands out from his journal entries, that for 25th October 1832 being a good example:

"On Tuesday I was obliged to go to Derby to attend a meeting of Gentlemen on the subject of the next Election – to me one of the most disagreeable of all unpleasant offices. I hate Politics – because they involve all the Bitterness, the Rancour, the Prejudice of Party: could it be possible for all persons to unite as Christians ought to do, for the public weal, I should then delight in them as cordially as I now detest them. To labour for the public good is – and I trust always will be – the greatest delight of my life. As to the next election, I can only put my trust in God and leave the issue in His hands, fervently praying that it may be for

His glory and the spiritual benefit of this distracted Kingdom".

Howard Colvin sums up Sir George Crewe perfectly:

"An able and serious-minded man with a strong moral conscience, he accepted his place in the affairs of the country, and devoted himself to fulfilling his duties as a Christian landlord and a country gentleman".

For part of his adult life – sadly quite short – Sir George kept some sort of journal, mainly detailing searching self-examinations of his behaviour and attitudes as a practising Christian. Much of this considerable output seems sanctimonious and contrived nowadays, easily mocked and parodied. But Sir George's agonies of self-reproach were genuine: his belief in God's will as applied to Christian standards was absolute. So painful and revealing were these reflections that years later many of them were heavily erased by his daughter, Isabel Jane. As she herself wrote in 1883:

"None but those who knew and loved him could enter into the depths of humility – the severe self-searching of his heart – it was all too sacred for strange eyes".

Happily, the journals contain rather more than repetitious expressions of religious anxieties. Here and there (and particularly in the 1830s) Sir George wrote accounts of his activities and of his reactions to the events of the day. Allowing for the circumlocutory style of the time, these provide a fascinating glimpse of the life and preoccupations of a country gentleman 170 years or so ago.

George Crewe administered his estates efficiently, and with compassion for his tenants. He took his public duties seriously, though chronically pessimistic about the state of the nation; during the 1831–32 Reform Bill agitation he really thought the world as he knew it was coming to an end, even though he was in favour of Parliamentary reform. In 1835 he became the reluctant MP for South Derbyshire, but never reconciled himself to living in London for long periods: his heart was always with his family and with Calke.

Sir George Crewe died on 1st January 1844, only 48 years old. The Derby Mercury reported:

"With deep and sincere regret we announce the death of Sir George Crewe, Bart, of Calke Abbey; a man whose Christian character – whose comprehensive and untiring benevolence – and whose unspotted private, and unimpeachable public, life have made him honoured and beloved by all around him ... Sir George was actively engaged only on Saturday se'nnight with his family in superintending his usual bountiful Christmas distribution of beef (the produce of three oxen), and other provisions, to the poor of Calke and Ticknall, and it is to be feared took cold upon that occasion, when it was remarked he had not for a length of time appeared in such good health and spirits . . . We do not wish to speak in terms of mere eulogy, but it is impossible to refer with any degree of justice to the character of Sir George Crewe without using language that, in itself, partakes of the panegyrical. We are convinced that we do but give utterance to the feelings of our readers and the public at large . . . when we say that a more estimable man, or devout Christian, than was the Hon. Baronet, it would be difficult to name . . . He was patron of eight livings, and represented the Southern division of Derbyshire in Parliament, being returned by the Conservative interest from 1835 to 1841, resigning the representation from ill-health. Sir George has left six children, three sons and three daughters. The eldest son, now Sir John Harpur-Crewe, is in his 20th year. Lady Crewe survives him".

The funeral took place in the chapel at Calke on 9th January 1844. To quote the Derby Mercury again:

"A large body of individuals – many of them tenantry – amounting to at least 1,000, resident at Calke, Tickenhall, Melbourne and the immediate vicinity, assembled to watch the funeral procession".

ACKNOWLEDGEMENTS

I should like to record my gratitude to the late Mr Henry Harpur-Crewe and to Miss Airmyne Harpur-Crewe for permission to use material held at the Derbyshire Record Office. I acknowledge, too, the help received from Mr Howard Colvin, Mr Roger Pegg, Mr Maxwell Craven and Mr Howard Usher.

My thanks are due also to Dr Margaret O'Sullivan, County and Diocesan Archivist, and to all the staff of the Record Office for their contribution over many years of research. Some additional material was provided by the Local Studies Library, Derby.

One other acknowledgement is essential – to my wife, who first suggested I should look at Sir George's journals.

COLIN KITCHING

CONVENTIONS

( )   indicates Sir George's words
[ ]   indicates editorial notes
. . .   indicates the omission of unnecessary words in journal entries

Journal of Sir George Crewe, October 1831.

Calke Abbey.   Painted by Sir George Crewe c. 1840.

SQUIRE OF CALKE ABBEY

[George's first attempt at a journal – of sorts – seems to have been in 1815 when he was being tutored (at the age of 20) by the Rev. Thomas Allsop at Fressingfield. The entries relating to George's penury at this time, and to his extraordinary relationship with his father, have already been quoted in the Introduction. An early page in the 1815 journal sets out the following rules for the conduct of his life:]

God has created me, watched over me and protected me to the present moment, placing me here to perform a certain part in the world. Therefore must I . . . show that I am thankful for the opportunity and means of knowing and serving Him, by doing it with unabated Zeal and Perseverance, with unwearied Diligence, with unshaken Firmness and Fidelity, and not only with Cheerfulness but with Delight perform the Task daily allotted to me, be it prosperous or be it adverse.

I must remember that next to my duty to God is the duty to my Parents, which consists of Obedience and strict performance of every thing that lies in my power to contribute to their Comfort and Happiness. This applies also to the rest of my Family and Relations.

Subsequent to this is my duty to my Neighbour, under which title are included all my fellow-creatures. To perform this part of my office I must let no opportunity escape me of doing any, even the slightest, good turn to another which may daily present itself . . .

I must struggle with unerring Perseverance (having armed myself with the precepts of the Gospel and keeping before me the Example of my Blessed Saviour) to fight the good fight of faith and resist the snares and temptations of Satan and the World, always endeavouring to keep myself properly employed so as to leave no unguarded moments for the enemy to take advantage . . .

November 25th, 1815. Fressingfield

Yesterday I received a letter from my dear Mother mentioning their safe arrival in Derbyshire . . . I immediately sat down, by the next post, to congratulate my dear Father on his safe return to Calke Abbey, nor could I refrain from expressing an anxious hope that I should be permitted to visit home for a short time, at least, before they again quitted it . . . O how do I long once again to embrace these dear Parents, whom now I have not seen for nearly two years. I have fancied that . . . I shall enjoy my next visit at home more than I ever yet did any previous one. But Ah! foolish fellow that I am, do not let me set my heart too much on these wished-for pleasures lest they should not come to pass. Let me see – it is four years, if not more, since I have seen either Henry or Edmund [brothers]. Perhaps my dear Father does not recollect that so long a period has elapsed since our last meeting . . . Time passes with a Person of his age apparently with far more velocity than with the young prig of 20.

Oh, how often have I wished not only that I could see my family more frequently – to whom now, alas, I am almost a perfect stranger – but that I could live with them.

[Editor's note: Further correspondence with his parents before the year-end did not produce the longed-for invitation to Calke Abbey, not even for Christmas].

December 4th, 1815. Fressingfield

About ¼ past two I went to Mills [probably a servant] to fetch my Gun and there I found, sitting by the fire, a Stranger with the hardest features and forbidding and repulsive cast of countenance I think I ever saw . . . He told me he was by trade a smith, but work was so dead he could get no employ – and, on having said this, relapsed into a silence which, joined to his bluntness of expression, would perhaps have repulsed all further Enquiries from a less curious Enquirer than myself. I then conversed with him about indifferent subjects, such as the hardness of the times, etc, etc . . . He declaimed grievously against the late prevalent custom of Establishing Iron-Foundries – said that they engaged nearly all the work – to which I replied "Yes, my friend, but still, as a great part of the Iron Work must necessarily be Wrought Iron, there still must (be) a considerable portion of Employment left for the Blacksmiths".

"Ah" said he with a sneer, "if they would take one part of the work, why should they take the other for me if I was a Master-Smith. Those who employ the founders to do one job should have their Horse-Shoes cast on to their feet before I would touch one of them". Seeing that this was rather a tender or galling topic I endeavoured to change it by asking some questions respecting his home, etc. To which I was answered that he had no home, nor had had any for some years – not for 11 or 12, I think he said – but went about doing jobs for this Smith and that Smith round the country, and sleeping at the Public Houses for the price of 6 pence per night.

I ventured . . . to ask whether he were not married. Yes, he had been, but his wife and he had been separated some years. He never would own her, nor ever put himself under her care again – not for one day, nor even a single hour, not he . . . He then went on to say that he married at Harleston [Norfolk] and had two Daughters. His wife turned out a Bad Character, sold or made away with every thing as fast as he brought it in. At last sold all she could and eloped with the money. This led him to his present unsettled way of life . . .

But had he not heard of his wife?

"Yes, time back a young man who lives at Withersdale Cross told me he saw her and my two Daughters at Norwich last Harvest".

I then tried to reason a little with him . . . and he, misunderstanding me, thought I wished to persuade him to live with her again and said with a marked and feeling expression very unusual in a man of his rank: "No Sir, I have planted one House for her, and I will never plant another!".

Having undeceived him he said "Yes Sir – I forgive her, if God can forgive her, but nobody, now we have been separated so many years, can make me own her, neither will I".

December 31st, 1815. Fressingfield

This year has been remarkable to me as a member of society, a subject of Great Britain, for the great and glorious victories which Providence has granted to the Allied Armies over the Usurper, Napoleon. This time last year he was meditating perhaps his Scheme of recovering France: in the course of 12 short months he has made his attempt, after having caused the death of thousands, and is now arrived at his State-Prison, the Island of St. Helena.

Whether this is to be the close of his career or whether yet he will be permitted by the unsearchable decrees of Providence to sally forth as a scourge to the world, God alone can tell.

March 4th, 1816. Fressingfield.

One thing or another has happened to prevent my taking up my pen sooner to make some remarks which belong properly to the evening of Friday. On that day, having ridden up to Harleston for letters, our post not going on that day, I found a very long and affectionate letter from my dear Father, the contents of which far exceeded my most sanguine hopes.

I had in my last communication to him expressed plainly and sincerely what were my wishes with regard to a future Line of Life after I left this place. I told him I should like, if possible, to set up for a Farmer, with such an occupation as would, from its profits, enable me to maintain a decent and creditable appearance – and there, with the exception of visiting my neighbours, would live quite a retired life. This under every consideration is certainly the kind of life in which I think I should be most likely to be really happy and comfortable. And I imagine also that it was probable this might be a Plan which would put my Father to the least possible inconvenience and expense, etc.

How agreeable was my surprise when ... I found that he not only seemed inclined to chime in with all my wishes but that the Proposals seemed in every way agreeable ...

[Undated entry – probably early 1816]

On Waltzing ... It is indeed a mode of dancing which cannot be practised without a violation of modesty, or at least a profanation of female delicacy which is highly revolting to every well-regulated mind. The close contact in which the persons of the parties must necessarily come is such which a modest woman cannot allow ...

[Editor's note: Eight loose pages were inserted in the 1815/16 journal and commonplace book. They contain George's account of his solitary horseback ride in June 1816 from Fressingfield to Peterborough. What the purpose of the trip was is not stated].

Monday, 11th June, 1816

Left Fressingfield at 10 o'clock and after riding an Hour and Three Quarters in a constant rain arrived at Diss, called upon Mrs. Allsop's Brother and dined with him. [Presumably Mrs. Allsop was the wife of George's tutor, the Rev.

Thomas Allsop]. After dinner set off for Thetford, leaving Diss in a drizzling rain, or as it is vulgarly termed a Scotch mist. I could pay but little attention to the surrounding objects, with the exception of observing that in general the Crops looked very luxuriant and the country well wooded and not quite so flat as most parts of Suffolk. The first village I came to was that of Bressingham, consisting of a few scattered Houses, at one of which, just on the turn of the road, I stopped to enquire whether I was in the right direction for Thetford . . .

A cart loaded with Earthernware was standing at the door. I asked the poor woman whether she was purchasing – she said Yes, if she could wish herself. I then asked her which Pot or Pan it was she had set her heart upon. The Salesman, lifting up a large red Pan, such I have seen used for milk in some of the dairies in Warwickshire, said "She would fain have this, could she spare the money". At which I gave her a shilling and 6 pence, being the price.

The poor creature was as much astonished as delighted and was thankful in the extreme, and the Pot-man said "Never could you have done charity where it was more truly deserved, for this woman has a very large family and is very often hard set to get a morsel of bread". I wished them good luck and trotted on with my head light and full of that delightful sensation which warms every feeling heart as having been able to assist a fellow creature in distress.

Soon I reached Lopham, remarkable for nothing but its Church which, something after the manner of a Cathedral, had its steeple in the middle instead of at the end. From thence to Garboldisham – narrow road so darkened with trees and high hedges that I had no prospect whatever.

On leaving this place I entered on the commencement of that wild part of country which occupies so large a part of Norfolk. Cultivated only here and there in patches, and producing nothing that I could see but Rye, Oats and a small quantity of Wheat, which looked very yellow and bad. A fine country for Game I should imagine. Passed at the back of a House standing isolated, as it were, in the midst of a Desert surrounded by extensive Plantations of gloomy Fir, which seemed to be the only tree this unkind soil would bear. I found it to be the property of Squire Thornhill, who is certainly making all the improvements the place is capable of . . . With the exception of three Cottages, which apparently belong to the Squire's labourers, I saw – I think – not one human dwelling between that and Thetford.

The Roman encampment and tumulus of that place first gave the welcome notice that my day's work was nearly at an end. Welcome indeed after a dreary, cold and excessively wet Ride of 18 miles, alone.

House, place unknown.
Painted by Sir George Crewe in 1816.

Arriving at Thetford I made strait down to the Bridge, intending to go to the Inn I had before visited and admired. But lo and behold, it no longer bore its former hospitable appearance, the entrance being blockaded by a pair of small Iron Gates which evidently were not intended to open for me. I turned round to a Bye-Stander who told me "That Inn had been long shut up, and that I had better go to the Bell". To the Bell I went – capacious House and convenient Yard – good Stable – Civil Attendants and tolerably good Larder. Here I drank tea, then walked out, following a path out of the Inn which led by the River side. A beautiful walk, the bank being planted with Alders.

Tuesday, 12th June

I liked my walk well, but to-day am suffering with a bad sore throat in consequence of my Folly . I slept tolerably well and about 7 o'clock on Tuesday mounted my Horse. No sooner had I got out of the town that I found myself again in the same open wild country with a road as straight as a line – neither hedge nor tree to be seen, excepting here and there patches of Dark fir. The cultivation appeared to be very irregular. The Crops of Rye looked well, being in the ear. The Oats were very backward, and what small quantity of Wheat I saw looked very wretched indeed. I saw several Ploughs at work, preparing for Turnip sowing. Five Ploughs with two Horses each in one Field, all in a line as regular as though they were marching in military order. This mode of Ploughing, with two Horses abreast, appears far more preferable where the light lands will admit of it. It is astonishing under what perfect command these animals are brought, and they perform their evolutions with an activity which would shame many of our Carriage Horses.

The only village on this stage is that of Elvedon, which stands like a luxuriant garden in a vast waste. Here the buildings, which seemed to consist of the Square's House and the Parsonage, seemed to be of great Antiquity ... Round this place you turn twice, the only turns in the whole road of 12 miles. A the end of the village I paid the first Turnpike since I started, a distance perhaps of 40 miles. All the roads, almost, in Norfolk are mended by Statute Duty, as it is called – that is, the Farmers work each so many days in the year, with their Teams, and since materials are plentiful and good, better Roads perhaps are not to be found throughout the Kingdom.

Leaving Elvedon I trotted on steadily almost satiated with a scene the novelty of which had at first pleased me. Here the patches of ground in Cultivation gradually diminished in number and ended at last in large Sheep-Walks and a Rabbit Warren. I met a Warrener with a true good Lurcher, and if I might judge from his load, he had had good sport. I should have liked much to have been able to take his portrait. A tall, stout, good looking young man with Hair and Whiskers nicely curling – not red exactly, but what the Suffolk people call "Sandy". His dog thorough-bred Black and Tan, with a ruff muzzle.

The next Persons I met with were two Shepherds with their dogs. I stopped them and enquired the size of their Flock. 500 was the reply, "sometimes higher up they have even larger flocks".

Not appearing very talkative I left them, and in about half an hour arrived in Mildenhall. The town is small, but neat and quiet. The Bell Inn tolerably good. Every provision for Man excellent, but for his Horse – miserable. Oats and Hay intolerably bad. The Church is very large and handsome, Steeple a fine height, the inside beautiful. The carved wood extremely curious, and in preservation excelling any I ever remember to have seen ... Over the North Gateway is a large room appropriated to the use of a School. The Alms Houses and Workhouse surround two sides of a Churchyard, very confined in respect to the Buildings. Close to the town is the residence of Sir H. Bunbury, or General Bunbury as he is commonly called. From the number of genteel people I have seen pass whilst at breakfast and whilst I am writing I should imagine it to be a good neighbourhood . . .

In about a Quarter of an Hour I found myself again the wild open Country, but tho' the outward Appearance was the same, yet in real Quality it was far more productive. On here the crops (with the exception of the peas which looked rather scrubby) were very good.

Passing through the picturesque and small village of Freckenham, I came to Soham, a large village with apparently good trade and thoroughfares. Here I bid Adieu to the neat white Houses and blue Tiles which had so universally attracted my admiration thus far, and entered upon the Ely [road]. Here I saw in a Field close by the Road Side, a field sown with something – but what I could not imagine. Luckily, before I got out of sight of it I met a peasant of whom I enquired. He told me it was mustard – "that it could be cut about a week before Michaelmas and that it grew a Yard and a half in height". To my question of what use it might be, he replied he believed they made oil out of the seed.

I now began to get a clear view of Ely Cathedral, I say a clear view for I had a glimpse of it very soon after I left Elvedon in the morning. After about half an hour's longer ride I found myself at the sign of the Lamb, Ely, a carriage with a launch Hood at the door. I passed it and turned into the Yard, but afterwards coming out purposely to look at it (being a chariot fitted up in the most convenient style for travelling possible) I saw under the crest "Byron". But a little surprized I eagerly enquired who came in that carriage to which the civil old Landlady replied that Lady Byron was upstairs at Dinner and would set off for Barton Mills very soon. Determined if possible to catch a glimpse, at least, of a Person who had excited so deep an interest of late I would not have my Rump Steak till they were gone.

[In January 1815 Lord Byron, the poet, had married Anne Milbanke, the heiress to a peerage in her own right. In the spring of 1816, soon after the birth of their child, Lady Byron fled from her husband and they separated for good. This caused a huge scandal, exacerbated by allegations of Lord Byron's unnatural sexual practices].

A large party were standing by the Door; I found means to put myself in such a situation on the opposite side [of] the Street that I could not fail to have a full view of the lady as she seated herself in the carriage – nor in this was I disappointed. "Rather small, of tolerable figure, with a very sweet countenance to my taste, dark arched eyebrows which gave her an interesting look".

I perhaps looked at her with more intent and less impartiality for the various reports I had heard with regard to the late unpleasant circumstances. And tho' I was pleased with her general appearance, yet with her manner I was rather dissatisfied. If she is really the woman of sound sense and extreme feeling that I have heard her reported to be, I think she might have shewn a little more delicacy in meeting the eyes of so many who were evidently on purpose assembled to gaze at her. A party of Cambridge men were there looking with as much curiosity as myself, and when she came out and saw the assembly of gazers I fancied I saw a smile of thoughtless gaiety in her countenance ill-becoming a person in her situation, provided she felt any regard at all for her late Lord.

The carriage having driven off I retired to my Dinner, after which at five, the Hour for Evening Prayer, I went to the Cathedral. The building is indeed magnificent and, in my humble opinion, exceeds in beauty Norwich. I was quite disgusted with the slovenly manner in which the service was performed. The chorister by whom I sat was improperly talking to me during the whole time the lessons were reading ... After walking about a little I retired to bed, having gargled my Throat with Port Wine Negus.

Wednesday, 12th June

About 7 on Wednesday I left Ely, passing over a rich luxuriant country with nothing particularly remarkable until I came to the village of Sutton which was graced with a Handsome Church and the highest Steeple without a Spire I ever remember to have seen; it must be visible 20 miles round.

Leaving this village I entered on a good road which brought me to the banks of the river Ouse, navigable from Lynn to Bedford – or the great 100 foot Drain as it is otherwise called. From here to Chatteris 4 miles and a $1/2$, as straight as a line, through a Fen, which from its sameness I now began to be a little tired of and was not sorry to reach Chatteris – which I did, very much fatigued. Having got an excellent Breakfast with very civil treatment, I called for a pair of Slippers, took off my Boots to ease my Legs and desired the Chamber-maid to show me now a Bed-room. I lay down between the Blankets for about an hour and a half during which time I got a tolerable nap. About $1/2$ past 12 I mounted my Horse, finding myself more refreshed by that short sleep than I had been by the whole preceding Night's Rest.

In about 2 miles I turned over a Bridge. I got upon the Road which goes along the Banks of the River through a country which gives the most complete Specimen of a Fen ...

The Mills by the side of the River for emptying the superfluity of water from the Level, into the River, were very numerous. I could count more than 40 ... The Bank is pretty from its commanding an Extensive View. Cottages every few yards, or rather wooden Huts, inhabited as I imagine by the Millers and Peat-Gatherers, numbers of which last I saw at work.

The novelty of this scene pleased me so well that altho' I walked every step of the nine miles I was not one Quarter so tired as I had been with the preceding twelve. I enquired of an old man who I passed on the road at what Price this Peat might sell. He said about 10 and sometimes 12 shillings per load. He said it made a tolerably pleasant fire to those who were accustomed to it. What I observed as most remarkable was the immense Quantity of wood which is dug out with the Peat in the highest Possible State of Preservation. Large Roots and Branches, and sometimes Whole Trunk of Fir, are dug up, of neither of which Trees is there a single living specimen now in the neighbourhood ...

I enquired at a Cottage Door (where I saw part of a large Body of an oak lying) to what use they put it. Sometimes, the cottager said, only for burning, but a great deal was good for "bulen housen" – building Houses, I suppose he meant ...

After my Ride at the Riverside was terminated I left this Line and turned up to the left, a mile out of my way to Ramsey for the sake of getting some dinner, and a bait for my Horse. Ramsey is a nasty, dirty, ill-built, poor Market Town, It was Market day and, excepting that there were a great many idle ill-looking fellows sitting lounging on the Bridge opposite the Inn windows, I suppose the town looked much as stupid as it must on other days. The George Inn I had been recommended to as the Head Inn, but so miserable was the outward appearance and so paltry the daub of St George and the Dragon that altho' looking about for it I had actually passed the House, not supposing it could be [the] place till, on looking round, I saw the words "George Inn".

Of all the ill managed and ill conducted places I never remember to have seen its equal: nothing ready, nothing convenient, neither did the master or mistress, if there were any, seem to know how to make it so, and – excepting the Hostler who was a clever sort of a fellow – there did not seem to be a servant in the House who knew their places.

I had the felicity of being waited upon by a Young Miss ... a raw giggling romp of about 14 or 15 who knew no more what to say in answer to even the plainest question I asked her than she would have done had she been as much a stranger as myself. She must go and ask what was in the larder, for she did not know ... The larder not containing anything very tempting. I then asked whether the Lamb and Beef, which I found had been dressed for the Markets Dinner, were yet cold. Here I thought I must have had a plain answer. But no, her treacherous memory failing, she was obliged to step back to the Kitchen to bring me word that the Lamb was not quite cold. The said Lamb at last I sat down to, and with respect to Beer, Newspapers, etc, etc, it would be wearisome to recount the blunders which occurred. I must not forget to state that there being no bell in the Room she thought it proper to pop her head, every 5 or 10 minutes, into the Door, asking whether I happened to want anything.

Having mounted my Horse after about two hours bait, leaving this miserable place, I started without having made up my mind whether I should go to Peterborough or only as far as Whittlesea that night. I rode along the Fen for a considerable way till I came to a Bridge with a Toll-Barr upon it, armed at all Points with Spikes. Here two-pence were demanded of me, and on my enquiry I was told the reason was it was what they called a Trespass Toll, the road being Private Property.

For the next three miles I went on very pleasantly . . . and then stopped – as I had been directed to do – at the sign of the Green Man to enquire which was the nearest way to Peterborough. A cross-looking female told me that, if I chose, I might go by Whittlesea, and if I did not like that I might go a nearer way along the Drover strait to Peterborough. It being a fine evening I preferred this last mode, apprehending the novelty would prove amusing . . . The country people whom I met stared at me as though I were a wild Beast, which plainly shewed travellers seldom, if ever, came that way . . .

The entrance to Peterborough by the London Road is very handsome. The River, over which is a handsome bridge, flowing through meadows where rich green gave additional beauty to the glassy surface which rolled majestically along, scarce ruffled by the slightest breeze . . . I rode straight to the Angel, a large and good Inn. A troop of 15 Dragoons had just marched in, as I was told, for the purpose of quelling a supposed riot, when in fact there had not been even the slightest disposition to such a thing. This had hurt the feelings of the respectable townspeople very much, as a talkative Banker told me, adding with much emphasis "You may believe me, Sir, there is not a more loyal little town in all England".

Thursday, 13 June, 1816

At 11 the following morning I attended Morning Service in the Cathedral. I scarce know to which to give the palm in point of beauty – this or Ely. The

Painted Ceiling here is, I believe, unrivalled. And the age of the monuments and building makes it rank high.

[Here, disappointingly, George's account of his journey comes to an abrupt end. The next journal entries appear in 1817 when we find George domiciled in Southampton – for unexplained reasons. The unfortunate young man is still no nearer achieving his heart's desire of living with the family at Calke Abbey].

August 10th, 1817. Evergreen Cottage, Hill, Southampton

. . . today I resume my Pen to record my accident. I was getting out of my gig in an Inn Yard when, just as I had placed my foot on the second step, the Mare lashed and caught me just on the left side of the Instep of my left Leg. Almost distracted with excruciating Pain, for a while I could scarce tell where I went or what I did. But when the pain had somewhat abated I retired to a room and sent immediately for a surgeon who lived, luckily, opposite the Inn. He examined my Leg closely and gave me the welcome information that all was right, no other injury having been inflicted beyond that of a severe blow . . .

August 25th, 1817. Evergreen Cottage.

Here I am still, without any prospect of an immediate removal, I am sorry to be obliged to say. Since my recovery [the only intimation that he had been ill], which I fear I have been too ungrateful for, my time has been spent but little in Southampton as I have been paying visit to friends in the country, making excursions to the Isle of Wight, etc, etc. And now it seems to me as tho' every former Habit which had grown upon my during my three years retirement at Fressingfield were completely reversed. Instead of Regularity, Confusion – instead of Humble Piety, Proud Hypocrisy . . .

   I spent the morning in serious and useful employment and then walked out to visit two poor sick people who ought to have been far more diligently attended to by me . . . In my ride yesterday I called upon them, and my conscience loudly reproached me when I found the rapid change for the worse which had taken place in each . . . One is a poor young woman, I fear too obviously in a rapid decline – the other a middle-aged man, somewhat similarly affected but I apprehend also dropsical.

[George walks over to Shirley Common, "in a lane leading to which stand both their dwellings"].

Cowes Castle, Isle of Wight.
Drawn by Sir George Crewe in 1817.

I found the young woman somewhat better. I had not a great deal of conversation with her, feeling hindered by the presence of her mother-in-law. When I went to the man's cottage I found him hardly so well – sitting, or rather leaning against the table reading a pious pamphlet which had been presented to him by a very good young lady who had visited him. I had never talked very seriously to him, and on this occasion perhaps felt unfortunately less fit so to do. However a few remarks I made, in a general way, alluding to the propriety of our considering both ways in which so serious an illness as his might turn out . . .

[The next journal of any kind to turn up is in a biggish pocket diary which George began on January 1st, 1819. He noted that he had not kept up a journal for the past two years. The entries in this small volume are necessarily brief, and cease in March as a consequence, probably, of the immensely busy and confused period George found himself in following the sudden death of his "dear Father" on February 6th, 1819. In the weeks before that traumatic event George visited friends at various mansions in Shropshire and Warwickshire].

Saturday, January 2nd, 1819. Condover Park.

I fear days spent in a visit at a friend's house must be more or less idly passed. Rode over to see Shrewsbury – day foggy and felt a severe attack of my Asthmatic complaint.

Thursday, January 7th, 1819. Condover Park.

Start to Shrewsbury, to attend the Oratorio – very much delighted. Dined at the Hunt dinner. Attended the Ball. Very genteel.

Monday, January 11th, 1819. Eatington.

Rode my new Horse, like him extremely. Must give up Hunting – it wastes so much time. I must think of returning to Hampshire.

[Eatington was the home in Warwickshire of George's great friend, Evelyn Shirley. The house is now known as Ettington Park.]

Friday, January 18th, 1819. Eatington.

Hunted at Mitford Bridge and went to Lord Clonmell to dinner. Tolerably quiet and sober.

Friday, January 19th, 1819. Eatington.

A delightful day at home. May God forgive me if I indulge a slight wish that I had not to return to a solitary, friendless Home.

Saturday, February 6th, 1819. Stockbridge, Hampshire.

Here, thank God, I am once again arrived in safety.

Sunday, February 7th, 1819. Stockbridge.

God's will be done. At past 6 o'clock arrived an express informing me of my Dearest Father's death by a fall from the Box of his carriage.

Friday, February 12th, 1819. Acklow House.

This day, thank God, I once more was permitted to see my dear Grand-mother . . .

Tuesday, February 16th, 1819. Acklow House.

Set off for Calke, a lonely journey, but thank God I arrived safe about 10 o'clock.

Wednesday, February 17th, 1819. Calke Abbey.

What a mixture of painful and pleasurable emotions arise on entering my paternal Home.

Friday, February 19th, 1819. Calke Abbey.

Who can tell what were the sufferings of this day. May God of His infinite mercy sanctify it to my profit. [The day of his father's funeral.]

Saturday, February 27th, 1819. Thomas's Hotel, London.

A noisy place but as comfortable as a London House can be expected to be. Well may I sigh for the country again.

Friday, March 5th, 1819. Thomas's Hotel.

One only day more in this horrid, nasty Hole. How happy shall I be once again to breathe the pure air of the country.

Friday, March 19th, 1819. Harleston [Norfolk].

With what feeling ought I to prostrate myself, with the deepest humiliation, for such blessings showered on me this day.

[Editor's note: This cryptic entry conceals the fact, I am certain, that on this day George proposed marriage to, and was accepted by, Jane Whitaker, whose home was at nearby Mendham. Their wedding took place on September 9th,

Jane Whitaker, Lady Crewe.
Watercolour c. 1820 by Octavius Oakley.

1819, in Mendham Parish Church].

Saturday, March 20th, 1819. Fressingfield (Suffolk).

Oh, with what still more agitated feelings do I visit this most delightful spot, the scene of my happiest, happiest days.

Monday, March 22nd, 1819. Mendham.

Returned here and spent a day with - - - - - - - - - - - -. [Jane Whitaker of course!]. Only too, too happy.

[Editor's note: The entries in this diary end on Saturday, April 10th, when George was staying at Penge Place, near Beckenham, Kent, where he had installed his mother].

[Editor's note: Although George does not seem to have kept a journal on a regular basis during the early years of his inheritance there is the evidence of correspondence to show that he found the business side of the Harpur-Crewe estate to be chaotic. With characteristic application he set about putting things right. And though over the years he gained the reputation of being a fair and benevolent employer and landlord, he was by no means a soft touch; an illustration of this appears in the following circular letter which was sent to George's Calke Abbey estate tenants very early in his incumbency].

Calke Abbey, October 16th, 1819.

Sir,

In consequence of my having lately inspected my Agent Mr Smith's book, I have become informed of an *amount* of Arrears of Rent from my Tenants large beyond all precedent and which under present circumstances, in particular, caused me no less surprize than disappointment. The Rent Day is nearly come round again, and but one or two individuals have made any tender of the money due.

Now it is my wish to shew every reasonable indulgence and encouragement possible to my Tenants, but at the same time I cannot and will not permit a system to continue which I am perfectly certain is highly injurious to the Tenants themselves, much less allow such a practice to be begun upon my first coming to my estate.

Let me only ask, if a man could not pay me £10 at Lady Day, what probability is there that he will be able to pay £20 at Michaelmas? And how is it likely he will pay me my Rent when it comes to 80 or 100 £? Were my Farms let at a Rack-Rent, the case would be different, but when they have always been let on the most reasonable terms such a neglect of payment is unpardonable.

I must, therefore, in a plain and civil manner state to you, as my Tenant, that I expect all Arrears of Rent (except in any case I may see ample cause for future indulgence) to be *immediately paid up*, and for the future must demand a more regular attendance on Rent-Days.

I don't wish to inconvenience any man, and where misfortune brings distress will always be ready to grant indulgence. But I must always think that, if a man cannot regularly pay his Rent, he either is not capable of managing his farm properly, or he lives in a way too expensive for his means, or too indolent to pay proper attention to his business, in either of which cases he had much better give up his Farm at once and take a smaller occupation than run himself into Debt, to his own certain ruin and to put me to the unpleasant necessity of enforcing payment in a way which would give me great pain to be obliged to do.

I don't wish to inconvenience any one when I can help, but I am convinced that if I permit a man to go on from year to year running himself into Debt I am in fact doing that man an Injury. At any rate, I am *determined* I will not begin with allowing such shameful arrears of Rent as I saw in the account of the last Rent Day brought to me.

I therefore shall be greatly obliged if you will pay proper attention to this remonstrance and not oblige me to repeat it.

George Crewe.

[The 1817-26 Commonplace Book contains a mixture of self-analysis, meditations, journal entries and correspondence. The lack of a regular record of what George was doing in the early years of his incumbency and of his marriage is particularly annoying; one has to accept that he was so busy putting his vast estate to rights that he lacked the time then to sustain the diary habit. One entry in 1821 stems from the fact that George inherited from his father the command of the Calke troop of Yeomanry.]

May 30th, 1821

"Casual Reflections upon and Narration of an Awful Event". Here is a quiet Sabbath at home, after a bustling and most unprofitable week spent principally at Derby where, altho' as High Sheriff I did not put on uniform, I still attended my Troop of Yeomanry Cavalry on Permanent Duty. The noise and bustle of Mess Dinners, the mixture of company and the entire worldliness of the whole concern, of course, were ill calculated to promote, in any degree, the practice of religious duties . . .

On Friday evening I had been to the Theatre, a place I never enter but on this occasion, and on my return to my Quarters at the Bell Inn, was about to take my Tea when Mr. Smith came in with the very disturbing melancholy intelligence that there had been a Fray between one of the Yeomanry, my non-commissioned Officer Henshaw, of Swarkstone, and John Somers, formerly in the Calke Troop and miller at Milton, but lately become Tenant to Sir F. Burdett [of Foremark Hall, near Repton] . . .

It seems they had drunk with too much freedom and almost without provocation the deceased Somers threw a Wine-Glass in the face of Henshaw, which cut him across the nose and under the eye, and bled considerably. Soon afterwards Henshaw enquired what Somers meant – whether he meant to insult him? To which he replied, Yes – he did mean both to insult and to hurt him, on which Henshaw answered "Then I think I shall return the compliment" and threw his Wine-Glass at Somers, which cut him severely under the left eye. He bled profusely; two surgeons were sent for. The Blood ceased of itself to flow, they plaistered the wound and left him, with the promise of returning before they went to bed, ordering him at the same time on no account whatever to stir from the Sofa on which he was laid.

But with this injunction he would not comply, but desired he might be taken into the yard to the privy. He was taken there, and sat a considerable time apparently in a doze. But before the drowsiness came on he had been in very high spirits and had shaken hands with all the party, said he was not hurt, and that it had only spoilt the look of his face.

Whilst he was in the privy a drowsiness came on him, on which his friends assisted him to remove [from the privy]. He did so and walked almost to the House Door when in an instant his Legs failed him and his two friends, Henshaw and Wayte, called out for assistance as, he being a very heavy man, they could not support him. With the assistance of the Hostler they carried him into the room and laid him down again on the Sofa, and knowing him to have been much in Liquor they supposed him to have fainted and afterwards fallen asleep – and it was not until Mr. Smith took hold of his hand, felt his pulse and his Heart and pronounced that all pulsation was totally gone that they discovered his Sleep to be the Sleep of Death.

In this stage of the business I went down to see the Poor Man, who was indeed a cold and fast stiffening Corpse. The medical attendants seemed unanimously of opinion that all was over ... Nevertheless all means for restoring suspended animation were tried, but wholly without effect ...

I enquired where poor Henshaw was. I found him on the steps in the yard, lying almost in a state bordering very near on insanity ... At last, by degrees, by perseverance, and more by God's Blessing and Aid ... we persuaded him do all he could to overcome his feelings, and, at length, we induced him to go with two of his friends to his own Inn "The Nag's Head". This done, I retired to my room.

Happily, on investigation of the Business before the Coroner, the Three Medical men who had attended gave it as their unanimous opinion, after examination of the wound, that it was impossible not only that the wound could have caused but even that it could have in any degree hastened his death; more probably it delayed it for a few moments. This their opinion was afterwards fully confirmed by the result of a surgical examination of the Head, the account of which I copy from one of these Surgeons (Mr. Hadyn's) own Hand:

"On the dissection, a very extraordinary quantity of blood was found in the Head, forming the most complete case of apoplexy I ever saw, and proved that, so far from the loss of blood occasioned by the wound being an injury, had he bled five times as much, probably he would have been now living". The verdict returned by the Jury was "Died in a state of apoplexy".

July 21st, 1821. Calke Abbey.

On Friday the great event of the coronation of his Majesty King George the 4th was celebrated at Ticknall by a dinner of Roast Beef and Plum Puddings to the poor men of Ticknall, in number about 500, when my Dear Wife distributed coronation medals to nearly 600 children of both sexes – 500 of whom on this day attended divine service at Calke Chapel, a most delightful and highly gratifying sight indeed. On this occasion, the small Chapel being crowded to an almost incredible excess we took the female servants of our Family into our own Pew . . .

November 25th, 1821. Calke Abbey.

Here again am I once more, by God's mercy, arrived safe at home after an absence of nearly three months in Suffolk, where we were detained by the short but dangerous illness of my beloved Wife. Her recovery is a signal mercy and undeserved blessing to me – a wretched, sinful, ungrateful creature who merits no such favour from the hands of my heavenly Father . . .

December 2nd, 1821. Calke Abbey.

Reflections.

I imbibed an awe and reverence for God, a delight in reading my testament and going to Church which was considerably strengthened by the excellent advice and example of my Dearest Mother and Grandmother – as well as by the advantages I then enjoyed of being under the roof of three tutors in succession, all pious men . . .

With these early good impressions I went to a publick School where under the guidance of persons of most excellent moral character, still I did not there see the one thing needful – certainly held up to me by precept and example as the only thing needful . . .

[George goes on to describe religion at Rugby School, including his confirmation by the Bishop of Lichfield.]

But as I grew older, rose higher in the School and became acquainted with all the Vice and iniquity so rife in publick Schools, good impressions had less weight, conscience was less troublesome, and when I left School I shudder to think how deep an inroad Vice had made in my wicked Heart. At this time, it being the wish of my Dear Father that I should not go to College, he chose a situation for me with a Private Tutor, the Rev. Thomas Allsop, [of] Fressingfield in Suffolk. This gentleman was of unusually austere, reserved disposition, and after having introduced me to two or three of the most respectable Families in the neighbourhood, shut himself up entirely. Not to this day has he ever seen company, excepting his Wife's Relations, and occasionally receiving the visits of very old and intimate College Friends . . .

At first the novelty of being my own master, the new style of country, etc, etc, occupied nearly my whole thoughts and attention. These were the hours of romance [as mentioned in the introduction, this was when George first met Jane Whitaker, whose father was Vicar of Mendham from 1788 to 1832], the first effervescence, if I may call it, of the youthful spirits. Ignorant of the World, secure from most of its temptations, there were happy, happy [days] – nay I feel, as far as worldly feelings go, the happiest of my days. By degrees it pleased God to give me Grace to apply myself diligently to Religion as a Study, and led me to frequent the cottages of the Poor as occupation in my leisure hours.

January 13th, 1822. Calke Abbey.

It may seem odd to anyone perusing this book hereafter (should it ever, when I am gone, fall into the hands of some idle and curious person) that there should be no minute of meditation or reflections on the entrance of a new period of Life [he simply means the New Year 1822]. I shall therefore *briefly* account for the circumstance – satisfactorily, perhaps I cannot because anyone would naturally ask the question "Why did you not take your Common Place Book with you?" . . . All this is undoubtedly most true. And the Truth tells much against myself . . .

I left Calke on the 2nd day after Christmas day, and arrived at Eltham Park, the residence of my mother, on the Saturday by dinner time, having undertaken this journey for the purpose of being present at an important meeting of Lawyers, previous to my sister Selina's marriage with Capt. W.S. Badcock

The Grove, Yoxford, Suffolk.
Drawn by E.J. Davy c. 1820.

[Royal Navy], as also to be present at that ceremony, which took place at St. George's Church, Hanover Square, at 1/2 past 10 o'clock on the 2nd inst. I visited my dear Grandmother, Lady F. Harpur, one day – spent three days in London and the remainder of the time at Eltham Park – and after an absence of 16 days arrived here about mid-day yesterday.

[As far as journal entries are concerned the years 1822 and 1823 are virtually a blank; spiritual reflections occupy most of the space. Yet a brief note in February 1823 states that George – and certainly Jane – have taken up residence at Yoxford in Suffolk, for unexplained reasons. An 1825 entry seems to suggest, perhaps, that the rigours of clearing up the chaos left at his father's death had so taxed a man whose health was always fragile that he had to get away from Calke for a long period of recuperation.]

February 2nd, 1823. The Grove, Yoxford, Suffolk.

About a week before last Christmas I left my dear native place – for, I fear, a long absence – to remove to this, my new residence . . .

[The lack of journal entries continues during 1824, 1825 and 1826, with the important exception of the birth of a son and heir – John, whose upbringing featured so prominently later on when George really acquired the diary habit.]

November 18th, 1824. [Calke Abbey].

This morning at 9 o'clock precisely my Dear Lady Crewe brought me a child – a son. From the previous delicate state of her health and also from the circumstance of our having been married nearly five years with but one hope of ever having that blessing, a family ...

My Dear Wife's Mother [Mrs. Whitaker] came down about 11 o'clock [pm] to speak to me ... She first roused me from my apathy by informing me that altho' all was right it was unusually slow ... Took to my sofa at past five and slept until a $1/4$ past six. No tidings. My fears were increased ... Began to dress afresh ... was shaving when I heard Mrs. Whitaker at my door, in a low and melancholy voice asking if I was there. Her swollen eyes and agitated manner almost petrified me. All was safe at present, she said, but no progress whatsoever was made for the last 7 hours. A consultation had been held between the medical attendant, the female accoucheur and herself – the result of which was they feared the necessity of taking those measures which, it was hoped, would save, if possible, the Mother's Life but must endanger the dear infant ... On my knees in the place where I had been standing, in an agony of mind I prostrated myself before my God and Saviour ... Instead of being exhausted by the agony of my mind I was calm enough to say "All is in the hands of God" and to resume my occupation of dressing. I had scarcely taken the razor in my hand when my dear mother-in-law burst in to my room saying "Thank God – the Child is come into the world, dear Jane is safe".

December 31st, 1824. [Calke Abbey].

Since the 19th of last month, from a variety of unforeseen circumstances my Dear Wife was again brought to an extremity of danger – perhaps in reality much greater than during her actual confinement ...

February 20th, 1825. Calke Abbey.

... When I left this place for Yoxford, 3 years ago ... If I speak the truth, I am bound to confess that so far from finding at Yoxford the leisure I had anticipated, and so far from leaving that place with regret that I should again be obliged actively to enter into the bustle of the world, I believe I never returned to Calke with greater joy . . .

November 18th, 1825. [Calke Abbey].

My Dear Wife and myself have just risen from our knees where we have been confessing our unworthiness, lamenting our past sins, whilst we commemorate the birth-day of our dear John and praise and adore the mercy of God vouch-safed to us at the time of his birth . . .

December 31st, 1825. [Calke Abbey].

. . . One afflictive dispensation we have been called upon to bear – the departure of Lady Harpur [his grandmother, Frances]. Not that we could for a moment lament on her account. No! She had filled up a full measure of a useful and pious life, and died peaceful in the hope that, dying on the Lord, she should also rise with him to everlasting bliss . . .

This year has been remarkable for the Health restored to my Dear Wife . . .

Our dear Boy has been spared to us in health and safety . . . Our servants and household have been spared – few have been ill and those, by God's mercy, have been restored . . .

October 29th, 1826. Calke Abbey.

A long time has elapsed since I opened this Book for its present purpose. During a part of the intervening time I was in a state of health which prevented my sitting at my Writing Table more than absolute necessity of business required. Since July I have been occupied in a very delightful Excursion into N. Wales, thence into Herefordshire, Monmouth, Gloucester, Bath, Bristol, etc, and a visit to my friend Shirley at Eatington Park – and since my return to Calke I have really had no leisure for much meditation . . . I am certainly much better than I was at this time last year, and I am far more capable of pursuing the duties of my station and enjoying that superabundance of domestic comforts with which I am blessed . . .

Bridge at Rhyader, Wales.
Drawn by Sir George Crewe in 1817.

January 31st, 1827. [Place not stated, but probably Mendham, Suffolk].

This being the eve of the anniversary of my Birth-day I seize the opportunity of a quiet Hour to enter upon "A Restrospect" of the year which is well nigh elapsed . . .

This period last year found me a great invalid, having struggled through the winter with frequent and severe attacks of Pain accompanied by a general Lassitude and Relaxation of Habit, which of course tended to produce considerable depression of spirits. Unable to take much exercise . . . I was principally confined to the Armed-Chair in my own Study. Early in April we paid an annual visit to this county. I felt refreshed by the change of air, and relieved by Relaxation from Business . . .

How little do we know what shall happen upon the morrow? . . . The arrival of an India letter in a few short minutes turned our domestic happiness to a scene of Grief, Lamentation and Woe by detailing the melancholy death of Lieut. John Whitaker, my dear wife's second Brother, under circumstances of course distressing, as well as from the length of time the event had happened previous to the fatal news reaching this country, as from the impossibility of making any particular enquiries concerning him . . .

We remained here nearly on the whole 2 months, not being willing to leave my dear wife's Parents until they had regained a tolerable composure of mind ... In May we left this place and proceeded by way of London to East Molesey Park on a visit to my dear Parent. Here we passed a fortnight very pleasantly and returned to Calke. It had been our intention to take a turn in some hitherto – by us – unexplored part of our country and to start early in June, but it happened that the annual meeting of our Yeomanry upon permanent duty was deferred until the 2nd week in June – this meeting I proposed to attend, but the Heat which afterwards made the summer of 1826 so remarkable had already commenced, and I felt entirely unequal to so laborious a task for an invalid. I was obliged to request leave of absence.

This being over we thought to start immediately, but it happened that the anniversary meeting of the Ashby Bible Society was in the next week, as well as the Summer Assizes quickly afterwards, on both which occasions I felt it my duty to try and attend. This being over we started upon our turn into North Wales ...

I returned home in September much improved and prepared for the winter. At Calke we found my dear Brother-in-law Whitaker, with his wife and child, come to us for a change of air, the former being in a very weak and precarious state of health. Also my Brother Henry returned from the Continent.

Here a fresh trial awaited us. Wright Whitaker alarmed us exceedingly and we could not contemplate the idea of his being taken from his wife and child, and that at a time when her interesting situation would render such a loss threefold, without deep sensations of a melancholy nature ...

Gentle exercise, and the bracing air of our Hills, with God's blessing upon the judicious treatment of Dr. Bent, proved highly beneficial and we had the pleasure of seeing him leave us early in December much improved in Health and Strength.

About this period another domestic event of no small interest took place – the accouchement of my dear sister Selina who presented her husband [Capt. Badcock, RN] with a bouncing boy.

April 1st, 1827. Calke.

I left home a few days before Christmas for the purpose of affording my dear Jane an opportunity of spending another Christmas with her own Family, and more particularly to spend that blessed season once more in the society of her mother, who had long been an invalid ...

We set off, in the month of February, on a visit to my beloved Mother, then residing at "Tring Park", Herts, which place she had taken for a few months for the double purpose of being near to my dear sister at the time of her "accouchement" and a change of air for herself. The weather was cold to a degree of intensity seldom met with in England – and so strong a contrast to the excessive Heat of the summer . . .

Nevertheless we found my dear Parent looking better and stronger than she had done for a considerable time . . . The cold became daily more and more intense – the House was old and not well-furnished, the rooms of a lofty and chilling size, the passages long and full of eddies of the merciless wind, which prevailed from the N.E. for nearly 3 weeks . . .

My dear sisters [Fanny and Louisa], and my own dear wife, felt the cold extremely, and our dear parent, also, suffered slightly from its effects – and I believe had nothing occurred to lay an embargo upon such a plan, they would all have left the House a fortnight sooner than they actually did. But as . . . it happened several things combined to prevent such a removal, and amongst other considerations "The wish of my dear sister that we should attend the Christening of her Infant" . . .

On the day of the christening, in the evening, my dear mother and two older sisters came up to "Turrett House" to tea with Selina. My dear parent was dressed in a Dress I had presented her with a short time before. She was in excellent spirits and, as I gazed fondly upon her much-loved features, I thought I had not seen her look so well for years . . . Within a day or two she complained of indisposition – we removed to East Molesey . . . and then she caught "a Prevalent Influenza" which had already attacked some of the Family.

A few days afterward was discovered . . . that her old and much-to-be-dreaded complaint "The Thrush" had made its appearance. At this time, having Business which compelled me to do so, I removed with my dear wife and child to London. We left Molesey upon Tuesday, the 6th of March . . . On Thursday, the 15th . . . I went down to Molesey – indeed should have done it sooner had I not been prevented by the Influenza commencing its attack upon me.

I did not see my poor Parent, for whether that she did not like to be disturbed or feared agitation, or had a consciousness of what state she was in, I don't know, but she requested that I should excuse her seeing me . . . She was very particular, however, in requesting that I wd. "not go far from her" – not farther than London . . . I hastened back to town, and having finished on the following day what little I had to do of business and having dispatched our dear child into Derbyshire, on Saturday, the 17th inst, I and my dear wife returned to Molesey.

Saturday night, Sunday night, Monday and Monday night, combined, constitute one of the most painful seasons I ever remember to have passed in my life ...

The dear sufferer, for some reason known only to herself, would not permit us to enter the room – that is, any one excepting her affectionate nurses Fanny and Louisa and a favourite servant or two. On the night of Sunday I went to bed early, but rose again at 2 o'clock to take my turn of watching in the anti-room. Once, for a minute as my dear sister Fanny went in, I opened the door wide enough to obtain a sad confirmation of my worst fears. It was the last glimpse I ever had of the living countenance of my dear, my beloved parent.

... On Tuesday the account was, I thought, a very unfavourable one. About one o'clock, having occasion to go up stairs to hear what was the last account, I went into the little anti-room for the purpose of obtaining information. I had not been there many minutes before Mr. S., the medical attendant, came up stairs. I had hardly sent him to the Bed-room ... when suddenly the door of the Bed-room opened, out rushed one of my dear sisters and threw herself into my arms, followed immediately by the other who also hung round my neck.

They did not speak, nor was it necessary ... I longed to rush into the room ... but I could not leave my sisters – particularly Louisa, for whom I felt great fear as to the effect grief so over-powering might have upon her tender frame, weakened as it was by constant watching ...

We remained with my dear sisters until the morning of Friday, when we took our leave and reached Woburn that evening – and on the following evening, by God's protection and mercy, reached our own dear home in safety ...

June 3rd, 1827. Calke.

Saturday following was the day on which it was expected the melancholy procession would reach this place. The intervening time was spent in the early part of the week in making many painful but necessary preparations. I found my malady increasing and my strength decreasing, and when the dreaded day arrived at last I was entirely unequal to going with my Brothers to Ashby, where it was settled we should join the funeral procession ... When the cavalcade was near I mounted a Poney and rode to the Lodge, and there entered the gloomy Vehicle (the very sound of whose creeping pace even in remembrance almost makes me shudder), joining my Brothers Henry and Edmund, and Mr. Jenney [William Jenney of Kings Newton, Derbyshire, whose wife was a grand-daughter of Sir Henry Harpur, 5th Bt.] As we wound up the hill, past the House to the Chapel, I thought I should have fainted away ... How I got through the service I know not ... On the following day I attended divine service at Ticknall church ... I returned home very unwell, and from that moment ... commenced the most serious features of an illness the most severe I have ever experienced – from which I am now ... I trust gradually – nay I believe in some respects I should say rapidly – recovering ...

The medicine of an Apothecary not doing me any good, Dr. Bent was sent for and certainly at first quite mistook my case, ordering me to live generously and take stimulants. This very soon cleared away the mask and showed the true complaint. A low Fever, intermittent, with a violent Affection of the Bowel.

What happened to me for the next 3 weeks I can hardly tell, altho I remember that I was in the night sometimes delirious with the Fever, that I had a nurse who sat up with me for a Fortnight and that "Mr. Child" [a surgeon] slept here every night during that time. And that, excepting shaving myself every morning (which somehow or other I never once omitted), I was entirely dressed by the assistance of my dear wife, my affectionate nurse ...

June 4th, 1827. Calke.

For six or eight weeks I remained in a sad state of weakness, altho by God's blessing the principal disease soon yielded to medicine ... I lived in my Bed-room and my Dear Wife's sitting Room. I was too low in spirits to hear or see any one for many days. I could not bear even to see my own Brothers. Our old and tried Friend, Miss Wheldon [a governess at Calke], sometimes came to see me – I believe to my Brothers' jealousy, but I found it true that, in great weakness, as there are no nurses equal to females, so is their society agreeable when that of men would not be tolerable ...

Like a child gradually imbibing new strengths, new ideas and acquiring new capabilities, so I daily and imperceptively ... acquired fresh strength.

June 10th, Sunday. Calke.

... The weather has been remarkably pleasant and I have endeavoured ... to spend as much time as possible in the open air and, I thank God, I have very great benefits from this plan. I began by rising early and walking half an hour ... every morning before Breakfast in the Balcony ... I found that not only was my appetite quite as keen as before but – if I may use the term – it was of an improved sort, more regular, not so ravenous – and I also found my Digestion better. Gradually for the last ten days I have made rapid progress in muscular strength as well as general recovery. My Stomach is rather weak and my Bowels have not yet recovered their proper natural state – added to which, from long inaction, my Liver has become a little torpid and I have been obliged to have recourse to Calomel in order, if possible, to rouse the secretions and produce their proper action . . .

July 29th, 1827. Lowestoft.

. . . I have been here three weeks. I came here chiefly for change of air for my dear Jane, but also with the hope that I might myself also reap some benefit from the refreshing Sea-Breezes . . .

When I first came here I was much disappointed in the place – thought the Lodgings very far from comfortable, their situation very unpleasant, and I subsequently found the place far less pleasing and attractive than other watering-places which I had formerly visited. What was the consequence? Why the real consequence was that I felt very angry, peevish, dissatisfied. Angry without cause, peevish without provocation, dissatisfied when I ought to have been very thankful.

September 9th, 1827. Calke.

This is the Sabbath-day. Our Chapel is under repair so that we have no service there and the afternoon is so wet that it is not practicable to reach any other Church . . . This day is the anniversary of that Happy time when I received before the Altar the hand of my dear wife. Eight years have now rolled away since that, to me, deeply interesting moment . . .

September 30th, 1827. Calke.

. . . On Tuesday last my eldest brother [Henry] was married at Newton Church [Newton Solney, Derbyshire] to his cousin, the eldest Miss Jenney [daughter of William Jenney]. It was a happy day to us all – very happy inasmuch as the union was not only approved of all parties related to us on both sides, but because it was formed upon grounds which give us every reason to hope the blessing of God will attend it.

[The following letter, copied into his journal, out of date order, gives a fascinating insight into Sir George's attitude to pursuit which he feels may lead people astray. The letter was addressed to Adjutant Cox, of the Derbyshire Yeomanry Company, "in answer to a communication from him that the Officers had, at their late meeting upon Permanent duty, agreed to subscribe for a Plate to be run for at the ensuing Derby Races by Horses belonging to members of the Corps"].

May 28th, 1827. Calke.

Dear Sir,

I fear you will have thought me long in replying to your letter relative to the Plate to be given by the officers of the DYC to be run for ... by Horses belonging to the Corps. It is at all times painful for me to differ in opinion from those with whom I am associated in any undertaking, and I feel particularly embarrassed at the Idea of being compelled to *dissent entirely* from any plan proposed by my Brother Officers in the DYC.

How far some of the Troops, which are composed of a variety of Persons in all Professions and all occupations in life, may stand affected by such a measure I do not know. But as relates to my own Troop, who are principally almost all "Farmers", plain, homely men who prefer to mind their Plough to dabbling in Horse-dealing – I confess I am not in the least ambitious to introduce them to the mysteries and fascinations of the Race-course, still less to encourage the younger members to imbibe a habit of Betting, which leads to gambling to a greater extent. Neither do I wish them to form acquaintance with Trainers, Jockies, Grooms, etc, etc, to whom they must and would go for information as to the Treatment of their Horses and other necessary points.

No; on the contrary, I would wish, as far as it lay in my power, to keep them from all such Temptation to Vice and Idleness ... I shall not bind my Troop under any command, but I shall certainly express my Hope that no member will think of entering a Horse. No one can be more ready than myself both to encourage the Breed of Horses as well as to stimulate the Breeder to continued care and exertion – and to any plan for giving any annual Prize to the man who comes out best mounted, on a Horse *of his own Breeding*, I wd. most readily contribute.

Or were a Fund proposed where from to assist former members, or those who had met with loss of a Horse or other misfortune to purchase a better Horse than they could otherwise afford to do – to such a fund I would subscribe largely and cheerfully. But by the plan proposed what will be done? Why exactly what has been done before in several Yeomanry Regts. and what is done too frequently:

some member buys a "Cocktail" just clear of being thorough-bred, good for nothing *but to run*, which will just carry him thro' the week of permanent duty and afterwards win the Plate.

I do not object more to the measure because I dislike a Race-course at all times than as I firmly believe it will injuriously affect the Corps as a body. Should this measure *spoil one good Farmer* by making him fond of betting and the Race-Course, I should maintain that an injury is done not only to the Gentleman whose Tenant he might happen to be but to the Corps at large ... On these grounds I must request the indulgence of my Brother Officers to allow me to decline subscription to the Plate. At the same time (that I may not save my money), if you will point out to me an Individual not in my own Troop who, upon small means, has always exerted himself to appear regularly and respectably, and well-mounted, I will send you what would have been my subscription to the Plate and request you to present it to him.

Believe me, Dear Sir,
Yrs very sincerely
Geo. Crewe.

November 23rd, 1827. Calke.

... I cannot suffer a momentary opportunity to escape of commemorating a signal mercy in the protection of Providence vouchsafed to me this day. I was out Shooting with my youngest brother [Charles] and, having beat Bryan's Coppice, we had called at Wicket Nook to visit the Home of Mourning, the Home of a poor Labouring man, by name "Cubley", who received a Fatal Injury whilst at work in my Stone-Pits upon Pistern Hill 2 days before.

This melancholy event, of which I had heard for the first time after I left home, had filled my mind with painful thought. Nevertheless I thought I would pursue my walk a short distance further. I had not gone half a mile on the edge of Pistern Hill, and was almost an equal distance of the fatal spot where the accident took place when, walking with my Brother, and not more than a yard wide of him ... I passed him – a few paces only – when in an inst. I heard his Gun behind me. I started, looked round and saw him on the ground, having stept in a Rabbit-Hole and fallen. The Fall had discharged his Gun, and the muzzle was pointed, I should think, less than a yard of the Spot where an instant before, I was. Had I kept my place, or had not his Gun – as it did – twisted quite round in his Fall, I must in all probability have received the whole charge which it contained at a distance of not more than 1 yard ...

Shore scene, place unknown.
Painted by Sir Geroge Crewe in 1816.

[Journal entries for 1828 are sparse. In connection with the narrative which follows, written at Southwold, Suffolk, George mentions that he had been away from Calke "in various places" for three months].

Sunday, July 20th, 1828. Southwold.

This is the second Sabbath since our arrival at this quiet and to me delightful spot.

August 13th, 1828. Southwold.

We have had thus far, for at least since the middle of June, a very unseasonable course of weather which has gradually got worse and worse as the season of Harvest approached. The late years of severe drought seem to be counterbalanced by an equal quantity of wet – and we who unfaithfully and ignorantly murdered at the want of rain are now seriously alarmed by its abundant, over-whelming supply.

The crop of Hay has been seriously injured – the rain fell in such torrents that even brooks, by general estimation small, overflowed their banks to an unusual extent and swept away the whole produce of Hay which had been cut. On the river Trent were two Floods covering the whole tract of Meadows, across which Swarkstone Bridge stands, in the short space of one week.

As I travelled to the Derbyshire Assizes the week before last, and returned last week, I saw many lamentable instances of the injury the farm had sustained . . . I returned from Calke to this place on Friday the 8th inst and upon Saturday occurred, for the first time under my observation, the melancholy sight of a "Shipwreck".

A corn-vessel, laden for London, and which only left the Walberswick Harbour the preceding morning, having sprung a leak of Orford Ness and being unable from the state of the tide to make Orford Haven, was compelled to run back for this place. By 8 or 9 o'clock on Saturday morning she was perceived in the Bay, showing signs of distress. Gradually she approached the Harbour but, having made much water and the sea running very high with a severe gale from the E:S:East, she dare not attempt the Harbour.

As the water gained upon her, and one Pump was choked, no resource was left but that of running her right upon the Beach under the Hope of saving the crew and cargo. This was effected about 11 o'clock, at which time I first heard of the circumstance and ran down to the Beach.

I saw the Vessel within about 50 yards of the Pier. By the time I reached her the crew were safe on shore, consisting of two men and a boy, with a passenger bound for London. The sea was tremendous – already it had washed all loose articles from her deck. The sails were torn into strips – her deck blown up.

For some time the raging of the waves seemed to bid defiance to all attempts at salvage, but as the tide turned the people began to busy themselves, and one or two having ventured on board, others soon followed. Every article was thoroughly soaked with salt water – many clothes were washed out and lost. The Books, Papers, etc, were wet, but principally saved. This being done, Baskets were provided and plenty of hands collected, by whom the cargo was soon brought on shore – wet and, I should think, quite spoilt. It was said to be worth almost £900 . . .

Whilst gazing around me. I observed a decent looking woman, in half-mourning, accompanied by an older person, walking slowly up to the Boats, in which were deposited such articles of clothing, Books, etc, as had been saved – and when she came to the Boats I observed that she burst into tears.

On enquiry I found her to be the wife of the man who had sailed in the Vessel as Captain. I spoke to her and tried to administer all the consolation I could by reminding her how thankful she ought to be that she was not at that moment a widow and six children fatherless.

I hardly finished speaking to her when a man approached from the wreck and came straight towards the spot where my dear wife, her sister and I were standing. As he drew near I discerned his weather-beaten cheeks grew deadly pale, his lips quivered, the unbidden – and dare I saw unusual – tears rolled quickly down his cheek as he slowly and hesitatingly, as it appeared, approached the woman I had been speaking to, and without saying a word grasped her extended hand and fervently pressed his lips to hers and said "Thank God Almighty".

The scene was so unexpected, and so touching, that I believe, of us who observed it, not one could refrain from dropping the tear of sympathy. Hastily he wiped his cheeks and returned to his occupation of rescuing his property, and I had a second communication with his partner. In the course of a few hours the vessel was a wreck – and the following morning the hull was sold for £12, to be broken up. All that remained of property which 24 hours before probably was worth £1,200!!!

September 21st, 1828. Calke

Here, by God's blessing, I find myself once again restored to my dear, dear home after much too long an absence from it. I returned into this county upon the 2nd of September – but only spent 3 or 4 days before I was called away again to attendance at our Triennial Musical Festival at Derby – a scene of more dissipation than is congenial to my wishes altho the intention is good, and I considered it a *duty*, incumbent on my situation, personally to support it ... I returned home from Derby on Saturday in the week before last and on Monday in last week we started for Buxton. I should not have left home again so early, but the season was growing late for the cold climate of the Peak and I was very anxious not to omit my annual visit to my Staffordshire Tenantry. Yesterday we returned home ...

October 5th, 1828. Calke – Sunday evening.

The last week was to me a scene of more bustle and worldly occupation than I could have wished. In the early part of it I was from home on a visit to my friend Sir O. Mosley, Bt. [of Rolleston-on-Dove], a pious and worthy man with whom it has long been my wish to cultivate a better and more intimate acquaintance. I believe it is right we should attend to the common courtesies of civilized society and should be thankful if we meet with those who, occupying an exalted station in life, are busily engaged in devoting their talents to the Glory of God and the benefit of mankind. I was much delighted with my visit . . .

December 7th, 1828. Calke – Sunday Evening.

I last night returned in company with my dear wife and child from a visit to my dear and much esteemed foster-parent (if I may so call her) Lady Skipwith, of Newbold Hall [at Newbold-on-Avon, near Rugby], Warwickshire. She was indeed a parent to me at a time when, but for her kindness and disinterested attention to a stranger, I should have passed a considerable period of my life almost without knowing what was meant by the relation . . . It is 20 years this Christmas since I first entered Newbold Hall, having been taken there by Mrs. Bloxam [wife of George's housemaster at Rugby School] during those Holydays which I was to spend under her roof.

Thus introduced, for six years I regularly spent all my vacations at Newbold Hall or with friends of Lady S. to whom she had introduced me. As regularly as the day of breaking up arrived, old William, the groom, with my favourite Taffy, the black poney, made his appearance and I trotted off to my new-found home as merrily as any little boy in the whole school.

When arrived at the hospitable mansion I had every amusement I could reasonably wish for. I had, in early times, 2 favourite Donkeys, afterwards my Poney – and during the last Xmas vacation before leaving school my friend William was my riding master. Staples taught me how to hold and load a Gun, and from Butler Webb I first imbibed the knowledge of Farming and Grazing in all their Branches. Thus were my mornings spent. In the evening I danced, played at Back-gammon, romped with then "little Selina Skipwith". Thus merry passed the fleeting weeks of Holiday, and when the last short day arrived, by whose sun-set I must return to Rugby, the kind wish always expressed "Well, *my dear*, we shall soon meet again" – accompanied by the bountiful replenishing of my otherwise empty purse – vanished the gloom of care from my countenance, more grave that day than usual – and it was not until I compared the narrow limits of my School Study with the spacious rooms at Newbold Hall that the frequent slight would at length find relief of (to me at that time) bitter tears.

Time rolled on, and I left Rugby. Even then I continued an occasional correspondence with my good Friend – and in about 6 years afterwards had the pleasure of visiting her in London . . .

January 25th, 1829. Calke.

. . . We held Service this morning in the Hall, most probably for the last time as – should it please God to spare us until Sunday next – we shall in all probability open the Chapel again. This work has been a long time in its execution but fully answers my expectations now that it is finished . . .

February 1st, 1829. 34th yr. Calke.

. . . This day is the Anniversary of my Birth . . . falling upon a Sabbath we had intended to have re-opened the Chapel which has been undergoing an entire repair and re-pewing, raising the roof, building a tower, etc, etc. For a year and a half it has been closed. But we have been prevented. I have been confined to my room for more than a week with a sort of infectious cold or Influenza – now very prevalent – and our minister, the Rev. M. Witt, is so severely suffering from a similar attack that he would not have been able to perform the duty . . .

[It was not until April, 1829, that the Chapel was re-opened, with George's ordained brother, Henry, taking the service].

June 24th, 1829. Southwold.

I have just been spending my Hour, as usual, with my dear Wife in reading and Prayer. When at home – Calke – sometimes I am unable to do it because I am called away to the discharge of my worldly avocations so soon as Breakfast is dispatched. When from home we seldom miss a day. A great comfort I find in this. We are united as one body temporally – why should we not be united as one soul spiritually?

[The place involved in the next entry is not stated but is probably Lady Jane's parents' home at Mendham].

8 mins. before 11 am, July 4th, 1829.

At this happy moment I was too much occupied to permit of my retiring to my room for any quiet purpose. I had just breakfasted when Elizabeth [Jane's sister] came down and said she thought the child was born – but in a few minutes she returned and said she was mistaken. In about 20 minutes afterwards Mrs. Whitaker rushed into the room saying with great agitation – The Child is born, the Child is born – and, embracing me with great affection, told me it was a nice healthy little girl [Henrietta Frances] and that all was perfectly right and well. My dear Boy was upon my knee and, tho unconscious exactly what had happened, kissed me with great affection and clung closely to me . . . So soon as we were permitted, I with my dear Boy visited the precious mother and child.

August 24th, 1829. Southwold.

. . . On the month being elapsed my dear Wife went to Mendham Church to attend divine service, and in the congregation to offer up her praises and thanksgivings for her safe delivery . . .

On the Tuesday following we took our dear infant to the Parish Church to present her at the baptismal font, she not having been previously named (no indisposition indicating necessity for such haste), where she was admitted a member of the Church of our blessed Redeemer by the name of Henrietta Frances Harpur. My Brother Henry, Mrs. Hulbert and Miss Lee, of Dickleborough [Norfolk], being the sponsors . . .

On the following day, accompanied by my Brother-in-law Wright Whitaker, I set off for Derbyshire in order to be in readiness to attend the Summer Assizes, held at our county town – which we did on Tuesday and Wednesday in the following week. During these two days we were inmates under the hospitable roof of my worthy and pious friend Walter Evans, Esq, of Darley Hall, near Derby – and much we both enjoyed an intercourse with a family in which God is revered, adored and worshipped . . .

On Thursday we set off for Ashbourne, where we took up our temporary abode at the Green Man Inn, in order to visit from there some parts of my Staffordshire Estates, etc. Friday was spent in a visit to Warslow [where Sir George built his Staffordshire retreat, Warslow Hall, in 1830] and Brown Hills. Saturday was so wet we could not stir out until the afternoon, when we dined with Col. Clowes at Yeldersley. On Sunday we remained quiet in our Inn, having opportunity of twice attending divine service.

On Monday we rode to Alstonefield to inspect the new Parsonage, as well as to endeavour to appease a certain dispute which had arisen between the Vicar and his Parishioners, or some of them. I have omitted to state that on the Monday evening before the Assizes I presided at a meeting at Repton for the purpose of establishing a Branch Bible Association at that place. We had a very

Village of Warslow, Derbyshire.
Painted by Sir George Crewe in 1841.

full meeting and therefore cause to be thankful.

To resume – on the day we left Alstonefield we returned thro Ashbourne to our friend at Yeldersley, dined and slept at his home.

On Tuesday morning we returned to Derby and thence to Allestree Hall to the Sheriff for the present year, William Evans, and spent Wednesday with him, meeting at his home an excellent Bishop (Ryder) on his circuit of confirmation. On Thursday we returned to Calke. My dear wife's mother – Mrs. Whitaker – we had left in very indifferent health, and we had received encouraging, but not comfortable, accounts of her. We called at the Post-Office, but found no letter, which alarmed us a little. As I anticipated, when we arrived at Calke we found a letter, via Ashby-de-la-Zouch, requesting we would return home immediately, as Mrs. W. had experienced a relapse and fears were proportionately increased. We got hasty dinner, settled all the Business we could and started in my travelling carriage, with a pair of Horses, about a quarter past six o'clock pm.

We travelled all night, halted at Leicester to drink tea, and at Newmarket the following morning to wash, dress and breakfast – and reached Mendham about two o'clock on Friday – having made an expeditious journey of about 21 hours, including stoppages – 148 miles. We found our dear Invalid uncomfortable, but not so ill as she had been. At six o'clock my dear Wife and I started in the Phaeton for this place to see the dear children . . .

We reached Southwold about 9 o'clock, slept here and returned to Mendham on the following day, Saturday. Much indeed against the inclinations of us both did we leave the dear ones, but having faithful and competent servants, we confiding them to their care and committing them to God, returned cheerfully believing we acted right in our arrangements.

We found Mrs. W. not so well, and on Saturday night we were alarmed about her – so much so that my dear wife was obliged to sit up all night with her ... This morning, as had been previously agreed upon, I was preparing to return home to stay with my dear Children when a message arrived saying that our dear Infant was *very ill, indeed alarmingly* so. We lost not time ... and reached this place about 2 o'clock. The House-keeper met us at the gate, saying the dear child was *better.* We hastened to the nursery, where we found the little dear in a sort of stupor, lying upon the nurse's lap and evidently more indisposed than we were aware of ... In about an hour Dr. Wilson, of Yoxford, who had been sent for, arrived – and immediately administered some calomel, etc, etc.

My dear wife was much distressed, and sincerely did my heart share all her parental feeling. Altho nothing doubting but that it was the will of God this affliction should come upon us – not hesitating to resign all to his will – it was not possible not to feel ... how strong the tie which in a few short weeks this dear babe had entwined around our hearts ... About 5 o'clock the dear child appeared somewhat more comfortable and the stupor seemed in some measure to subside and, altho the first medicine – which included Calomel – had twice been rejected by the Stomach, since that some other medicine had been retained and a portion of food had been taken with some apparent degree of appetite ...

August 25th, 1829. 2 o'clock pm. Southwold.

Once in the night I got up, my dear wife thinking our precious babe not quite so well. The increased indisposition, however ... was, thank God, only temporary. On the whole I thought her better and she, thank God, continued so untill now, when a slight return of inward pain has shown itself, and the stomach evidently does not like the powders which are given. My dear wife was dreadfully low and much oppressed this morning, but we prayed together ...

Having been much from home since my dear wife's confinement I had scarcely identified the dear child as my own – certainly with shame and penitence do I humbly confess I had not estimated it as the gift of God – and very often when sauntering in the dell at Mendham, in silent meditation, how deeply did I grieve at the coldness and dullness of my hard heart . . .

August 26th, 1829. 9 o'clock pm. Southwold.

This evening my dear partner, having retired early in order to recruit herself after 2 nights watching over our dear Babe, leaves me in solitude . . . The dear object of our mutual anxiety is much recovered . . .

September 4th, 1829. Southwold.

. . . Yesterday morning, about 7 o'clock, I was suddenly called up . . . to the nursery, where I saw the body of our dear Infant, but the spirit had winged its Flight – I think and believe – to Heaven. She had never been materially better, and now it is probable that, altho unperceived by us, the disease – which appeared to be a bilious attack – had gradually worked its course to a sure and fatal conclusion . . . Her dear little face appeared as tho she was still sleeping, and her little hands were closed in the same easy way in which she always held them when asleep . . .

To describe first feelings on such an occasion were fruitless . . . I feel it to be the judgement of God, but as a believer in Jesus Christ I hope it is also a loving messenger of ultimate mercy . . .

September 7th, 1829. Southwold.

. . . At 10 o'clock this morning my dear wife and I, accompanied by our dear John and my brother-in-law George Whitaker, followed the remains of our dear Infant to their last home. In the Chancel of this beautiful Church, nearly close to the door, on the right hand side as you enter in, was deposited the relic of frail mortality. It was our earnest wish to avoid all "pageantry of grief". Six girls, daughters of our Trades-people, neatly dressed in white, were bearers. The Rev. H.R. Birch, the rector, and Mr. Sutherland, the surgeon, walked before them and we were followed by 4 of our maidservants.

It was a melancholy tho short procession, and to my dear wife it was the more trying because it was the first time in her life that she had ever attended a Funeral. Strange curiosity brought numbers of children and young people about us, and their noise and vivacity was to me something surprizing. Nor were they even quiet when arrived in the Church, but required the frequent attention of the Sexton and Beadle to keep them in a state of decent order.

September 12th, 1829. Mendham.

Yesterday afternoon, $^1/_2$ past 4 pm, we left Southwold upon our return ... homewards. It was naturally to be expected that such an event would powerfully tend to renew our grief. My dear wife was much distressed. I kept up my tranquillity untill as we passed thro the end of the town I turned my head to take one peep more at the Church where I was about to leave behind the mortal remains of my dear infant. This quite overwhelmed me, and I found it quite impracticable to restrain the flow of natural feeling. On our arrival here I found many letters of condolence from kind and affectionate relatives and friends – these opened the wounds afresh.

[The next dated entry is November 8th, 1829, at Calke].

December 19th, 1829. Hastings, Sussex.

... Here I am, for the first time at this season of the year, away from my home and home duties. Not without considerable and real reluctance have I persuaded myself so to do. My health – altho, praise be to God, much restored – has yet suffered much for several years past from a species of Rheumatic Cramp or Neuralgic Spasm, as the doctors term it, allied too closely to a species of incipient Tic Douleureux. I have always suffered much from this in the winter season, and at Calke – partly from, I think, the cold dampness of our climate there, and partly, as I have now reason to believe, from the over-exertion of my mind in various business when at home, and an accompanying neglect of or incapacity of leisure for proper exercise out of doors. For the cure of this a winter's residence in a warmer climate has frequently and strongly been recommended to me ...

This place has its many and melancholy warnings. We have only been 4 days in this place and two victims of early disease have been carried to their graves amongst my near neighbours. One – I don't know who – a child, the other in prime of youth, the sister of the present Marquis of Lothian ...

[Sir George made an unfortunate choice of a winter to spend on the Sussex coast. The weather turned out to be exceptionally severe, with low temperatures and repeated falls of snow].

Saturday, January 2nd, 1830. Hastings.

In the morning pursued my course of reading with my dear Jane, and afterwards took a long walk, returning home thro St. Leonards new town. The country pretty, but apparently thinly inhabited. The weather continues very severe. A partial thaw under the Cliff, but on the high-ground very little symptom of change. Wind NW, very cold with a mist on the high-ground . . .

Monday, January 4th, 1830. Hastings.

. . . About mid-day rode for an hour or two upon the Sands. At past 5 dined at Mr Canne's – much against my will – meeting Lord Eglington, Miss Curtis Barton, Sir W. Waller, etc, etc. In the evening a rout took place at the same house. A curious motley group – as motley in Character as in dress and figure. Wonder much in what the pleasure of such a meeting consists. I wish in vain to penetrate the mystery.

Wednesday, January 6th, 1830. Hastings.

. . . Rode with my friend Col. Clowes towards Bexhill and upon the sands – the road being still too hard. Then walked with my dear wife to call upon Lady Lavington. My old School-master Archdeacon Goodenough called upon me. Dined quietly at home, envying no Rout-goer.

Saturday, January 9th, 1830. Hastings.

Read at home in the morning as usual. Then walked with my dear wife – really almost like a spring morning. The sea looked calm and blue. Then accompanied my friend Col. Clowes to see a new instrument invented by – Ronald, Esq. for drawing correct Perspective . . . Heard of the death of Sir Thos. Lawrence, suddenly on Thursday last. Vanity of Vanities! All is vanity. How short a warning!

[Sir Thos. Lawrence, the portrait painter, who had an interesting connection with the Harpur family. As Howard Colvin mentions, Lawrence was the son of an innkeeper at Devizes. Sir George's grandfather, Sir Harry, and Lady Frances came across his talent en route for Bath and so admired it that Sir Harry offered to pay for the young man's artistic education in Italy. Lawrence's father refused the offer, but the early connection is reflected through the pastel portraits of Sir Harry and his son which hang in the Drawing Room at Calke].

Sunday, January 10th, 1830. Hastings.

. . . Decided not to go to the Sessions at Derby, as I had intended. I pray God for direction. I would not spare myself trouble, but for many reasons judged it best, as far as I could see, to abandon the idea . . .

Monday, January 11th, 1830. Hastings.

Heavy fall of snow. Read as usual. Wrote letters, and proceeded with my Letter on the Game Laws ... Begin to rejoice that I did not pursue my intended journey into Derbyshire.

[Sir George took the view that it was the custom of rearing game on big estates which tempted poor people to indulge in poaching, and so to fall foul of the harsh Game Laws. He sought to persuade landowners to abandon the practice – with the consequence (he thought) that in due course the need for the Game Laws would be eliminated].

Tuesday, January 12th, 1830. Hastings.

. . . Took a walk in spite of the falling snow. Found a sheltered spot where I was enabled to get my usual exercise . . . The weather more severe than has been since 1813-14 . . .

Wednesday, January 13th, 1830. Hastings.

A very heavy fall of snow. Untill one o'clock could not possibly get out. At last ventured out, and endeavoured to reach the East Hill – but found the snow drifts so deep, and the storm so violent, that at last I was obliged to turn back.

Thursday, Janaury 14th, 1830. Hastings.

Read at home all the morning. Then took a long walk through snow and snowdrifts ... The cold so intense that, altho in strong exercise, my right ear was frozen . . .

Friday, January 15th, 1830. Hastings.

. . . At mid-day, altho it snowed hard, walked about 3 miles up to the Fish-Ponds . . . Snowed and froze alternately all the afternoon . . .

Saturday, January 16th, 1830. Hastings.

. . . Wrote a long letter to my dear Brother Henry upon Calvinism, explanatory of my reasons for not approving it . . . Froze hard again this afternoon. The coldest day I ever remember to have felt for many years . . .

Tuesday, January 19th, 1830. Hastings.

. . . Walked to see the Falls, called the "Old Roars", about 3 miles north west. Found it frozen, the effect very pretty . . .

Wednesday, January 20, 1830. Hastings.

A sudden thaw took place early this morning, the wind having changed to E.S.E. Blew a hurricane all day. Read as usual, could not go out . . .

Thursday, January 21st, 1830. Hastings.

. . . A poor French Fishing Boat was lost here in the gale. It is supposed and feared all hands lost. Went with my dear wife to Mrs. North's dance. A very quiet, agreeable evening. In moderation I think dancing by far the best amusement for young people.

Friday, January 22nd, 1830. Hastings.

Read as usual in the morning, wrote some letters. Then walked in search of a poor Widow whose husband died suddenly at Brighton immediately upon landing and taking off his Fisherman's Boots. He had been ill some time and was out 3 nights in the late severe gale of wind . . .

Thursday, January 28th, 1830. Hastings.

. . . Mounted my horse and took a ride in the lanes. Found them very muddy in the valleys, but hard frozen on the hills and where exposed to the N.E. wind, which blew piercingly cold. Accompanied Elizabeth Whitaker to a dance at Mrs. North's – very pleasant evening.

Saturday, January 30th, 1830. Hastings.

. . . A heavy Fall of Snow again last night. Walked thro the most wretched mass of snow and mud, with my friend Bell, to St. Leonards . . . It blows hard tonight with Heavy Fall of Snow. This is indeed a severe winter . . .

Wednesday, February 3rd, 1830. Hastings.

. . . The day was not favourable for walking – snow and with frost. The most severe winter in the South. In the North, according to reports, by no means so . . .

Friday, February 5th, 1830. Hastings.

. . . Walked with Bell over the hills in search of a poor woman in distress. Found her – a delightful picture of cleanliness, neatness, patience and good economy. Snowed fast as we returned home . . .

Saturday, February 6th, 1830. Hastings.

. . . Wrote letters and in my common-place book. Then walked by myself to see the poor woman again. This severe weather and the hardship of the times multiplies the objects of pity daily.

Wednesday, February 10th, 1830. Hastings

Was prevented reading this morning, my dear Jane being occupied with the Child, Sadler [the nurse] being very unwell. Accompanied her [Jane] and my friend "Bell" to Mrs. Smith's in the evening. How tired the Hastings people must be of seeing each others' faces day after day at the same dull routs.

Sunday, February 14th, 1830. Hastings.

. . . My friend B. J. Bell left us to-night, per mail – cannot but feel at parting with so tried and valued a friend . . .

Monday, February 15th, 1830. Hastings.

Read to myself in the morning. Afterwards rode with Eliz. Whitaker to Bexhill, etc. Day cold and comfortless. Enjoyed the exercise, however. Cannot divest myself of the idea that Fog and Gloominess of Weather is more prevalent in the vicinity of the sea than elsewhere. Miss my friend Bell exceedingly.

Tuesday, February 16th, 1830. Hastings.

Having had but little exercise of late, determined to have a good ride. Started at 11 o'clock and rode to Pevensey and Eastbourne. Pevensey castle – fine ruin. E-Bourne – the village very pretty . . .

Saturday, February 20th, 1830. Hastings.

. . . Took a lesson in oil colouring from Mr. Mouchet – a very clever, sensible German artist. Wish I had found him before.

Monday, February 22nd, 1830. Hastings.

. . . This evening the house was thrown into alarm by a thief being caught in our garden, after having paid us several visits, no doubt! Believe him to be in distress, but idly – and unwilling to support himself in a reputable manner.

Thursday, February 25th, 1830. Brighton.

Left Hastings this morning, accompanied by my friend Lieut. Col. Clowes, to visit our mutual friend Sir Robert Wilmot [of Chaddesden Hall, Derby, but on holiday in Brighton], via Battle, Horsebridge and Lewes . . .

Friday, February 26th, 1830. Brighton.

Spent the greater part of the morning in walking round this enormous overgrown place with my friend – in search of a House for his residence during the summer. Dined with Sir Robert . . . But for its size I think I should like Brighton better than Hastings.

Saturday, February 27th, 1830. Hastings.

Returned from Brighton to-day.

Wednesday, March 3rd, 1830. Hastings.

This being the day previous to our departure, all was necessarily bustle and confusion ... took leave of Lady Lavington – perhaps I may never see her again. Have been disappointed in the cold-hearted worldliness of the Hastings people.

Thursday, March 4th, 1830. Seven-Oaks, Kent.

Left Hastings this morning, a little after 11 o'clock ... Cannot say I felt any deep regret at leaving Hastings – the Place is quite spoilt by the Influx of gay company in the winter season.

Saturday, March 6th, 1830. Brunswick Hotel, Jermyn Street, London.

London is to me a hateful place, unless I had a comfortable quiet house of my own, where I could be surrounded with my usual occupations ...

Monday, March 8th, 1830. Brunswick Hotel.

Walked out early – shopping, etc. .... This evening Mr. Whitaker and Wright Whitaker arrived per coach from Norfolk to meet my dear wife, she not feeling equal to an additional journey of so great a distance.

Wednesday, March 10th, 1830. Brunswick Hotel.

Accompanied by my Father and Brother-in-law went to Thomas's the dealer in Horses, Park Lane. Agreed for the exchange of one of our Horses and purchase of another. Almost wish, as times are, that I could do without such luxuries – but then, what would the Farmers do who breed Horses? Believe one ought to share one's wealth as equally as possible amongst all classes.

Monday, March 15th, 1830. Calke Abbey

Left Northampton this morning about 10 o'clock. Took an early dinner at

Leicester and reached home about six o'clock . . .

Wednesday, March 17th, 1830. Leylands, near Derby.

Drove with my Brother-in-law, Wright Whitaker, to Derby. Mounted my horse and rode to meet the Sheriff, R. L. Newton, Esq. Dined with him at the King's Head. Rode out to meet the Judges. Afterwards came to this pretty place on a visit to Mr. W. Newton.

Thursday, March 18th 1830. Leylands.

At 11 o'clock rode to Derby. At 12 attended in court to serve upon the Grand Jury. Sat until half past five o'clock. At six dined with the Judges – Alexander and Garrow – returned, tired, to this quiet and agreeable home. Enjoyed a quiet evening with Mr. Newton.

Friday, March 19th, 1830. Leylands.

At 9 o'clock attended upon the Grand Jury. Sat untill half past 4 when we were dismissed. Went to the Bell Inn where I transacted business with my Stafford-shire agent . . . Came here to dinner and passed another very agreeable evening.

Saturday, March 20th, 1830. Calke.

Returned home about 1/2 past 1 . . . Am delighted to return to my own dear home . . .

Tuesday, March 23rd, 1830. Calke.

Was engaged with Mr. Smith [Sir George's Calke estate agent], etc, all this morning untill one o'clock. Mounted my horse and rode over to Repton Park to dine with my Brothers Edmund and Charles . . .

Wednesday, March 24th, 1830. Calke.

Went to my office at 10 o'clock and was engaged in magisterial business untill 1/2 past one o'clock. We dined at two o'clock. Persons on business kept me at home untill 5 o'clock. Mounted a poney and enjoyed a delightful evening's ride over my farm, etc.

Calke Abbey.   Drawn by Eyre, date unknown.

Thursday, March 25th, 1830. Calke.

Mr. Sheffield, surgeon of Ticknall, came to me on business and detained me until ½ past 11 o'clock. Walked to inspect my Flocks and Herds till two. At two Mr. Smith dined with me, Lady C. being gone to Repton Park . . .

Monday, March 29th, 1830. Calke.

. . . The weather for the last 2 days or 3, to-day inclusive, has been hotter than I ever remember in my life at this season of the year. Thermometer 80 in the shade.

Wednesday, March 31st, 1830. Calke.

At 11 o'clock rode to Repton to attend the Magistrates' meeting. Found only Sir O. Mosley there. Had a long and tedious day's work and rode home in a pouring Rain . . .

Friday, April 2nd, 1830. Calke.

To-night [Sir George must surely mean "last night"], to our surprize, it began to snow. Snowed without interruption untill this evening at about sun-set. The Snow in some drifted places four or five feet deep. On the land, nearly 8 inches . . .

Saturday, April 3rd, 1830. Calke.

Sharp frost last night and bitterly raw and cold to-day. Snow thawed rapidly in the sun. Did not stir out, excepting to my office . . .

Monday, April 15th, 1830. Calke.

Rode to attend the Sale of poor Lord Tamworth's effects at Batt House. Snow gradually going – a fine day. I was made melancholy by contemplation of the untimely death, by his own habitual intemperance, of poor Lord Tamworth. Strange that 2 of that Title successively should have fallen victim to Intoxication.

Wednesday, April 7th, 1830. Calke.

Rode – much against my will – to attend the general meeting of Governors at The Derby Infirmary. A strong proceeding – much bad blood still stirring, and the consequence – want of cordiality, want of mutual confidence. Adjourned at 4 o'clock, having done little or nothing.

Saturday, April 10th, 1830. Calke.

Was engaged in the morning with persons upon Business . . . In the evening a person by the name of Edwards came up to play upon the Musical Glasses. Evidently a clever man, and with a strong passion for music.

Wednesday, April 14th, 1830. Calke.

Was engaged in Magistrates' Business in the morning. Spent an hour in the garden, directing grafting trees, etc. Dined at 2 o'clock. In the evening rode down to Ticknall, called on some of my neighbours . . .

[Editor's note: This particular diary ends at that point. It overlaps, in part, the journal from which various entries have been taken – eg: those concerning the birth and tragic early death of Henrietta. Further entries from this journal now follow].

June 4th, 1830. Calke.

12 o'clock night. Within 24 hours of eleven months only past did I sit down for the same purpose and on the same occasion upon which my Pen is at this moment to be employed. As it will be seen by reference to the former pages of this book it was on the night of the 4th July 1829 that my dear wife was first taken ill previous to the birth of our last dear infant, and upon the 3rd September that it pleased God, in his unerring wisdom, to take to himself the precious gift . . .

1 o'clock. I was called out of the room about 1/2 an hour ago by information that Mr. Godwin, the accoucheur, was arrived – a relief to me because, as he lives 10 miles from home and we only sent for him about 9 o'clock. I was very anxious to hear something of his arrival.

1/2 past 2. Having to entertain Mr. G. and my Brother-in-law [Wright

Whitaker] being still up, I cannot sit down to write, as I could wish . . . My dear wife, when I saw her last, said "Pray for me – I know you will".

5 mins past 7 am (June 5th). I had sat up with Wright Whitaker in the Library, and at past 6, feeling very weary, had lain down upon the sofa and was dosing [sic], but not asleep, when Anna Whitaker [Wright's wife] came in and announced that my dear wife had got a "nice little girl" [Isabel Jane] – that she had suffered extremely, more than at her last confinement, but was not much exhausted . . .

I have just had the extreme delight of seeing my dear wife – and her lovely babe – she told me she was not much fatigued, but her countenance betrayed the contrary . . .

Saturday, June 26th, 1830. Calke.

The event of last night was so far remarkable that some record of it is worthy of being kept . . . On Friday, in the morning, it began to drizzle with rain . . . and continued to do so untill night when, about 7 o'clock, it partially ceased but the clouds collected in dense and dark masses . . . About 1/2 past nine o'clock I first heard distant thunder which presently appeared to approach Calke. The Lightning . . . was incessant and extremely vivid.

About 10 o'clock the storm became so threatening to be very severe that I thought I would defer our assembly for Evening Prayers for a while. About 20 minutes after 10 it appeared to abate a little, when I rang the Bell for Prayers . . . From that time, except sharp flashes of Lightning now and then, all was quiet untill about 11 o'clock when I went upstairs to bed. My dear boy sleeping in his crib by my bed-side I thought it best to close the shutters and draw the curtains – which having done, I sat down to read the new Edition of "The Pilgrim's Progress".

About 1/2 past 11 the rain began to fall in *torrents* – I might say to descend in one sheet of water. Such rain I never before heard . . . Thus it continued, I should think, for at least an hour and a half. About 1/2 past one it principally subsided, and I being on my knees, thanked God for his merciful preservation of myself, my family and household and retired to rest, and slept soundly until 7 o'clock this morning.

So soon as I was dressed I had curiosity to go out and see the effects of the storm. The morning was fine, all was calm . . . I went down stairs to my Study. The first thing which attracted my attention, as I left the Saloon, was the noise of the Buckets, Pattens, Brushes, etc, etc, and numerous voices below. I hastened down and found that the water had penetrated the front lower door, had filled the passage on the ground floor and my Anti-room – and made its escape into a Bed-room . . . Here was a scene of confusion, the Mats and Carpets saturated with Red Mud – and the boards soaked.

I walked out and found the grass plot in front of the House, and the carriage-drive, etc, in a most woeful state. A large portion of the grass plot was covered in at least 5 inches, or six, with Stones and Gravel, the Pavee was 2 inches deep in a settlement of Red Marl, and the road was washed entirely to its foundations, with in many places deep gullies cut by the merciless stream. Three or Four carts and teams, with 8 or 10 men, were employed, and have been the whole day, in carrying back the gravel, levelling the road and clearing the Pavement.

At 11 o'clock I went to the Petty-Sessions at Ashby with very considerable difficulty . . . I believe as severe a flood has been seen, but never in my recollection; nor in the recollection of any person I have yet seen has there been an instance of so much rain falling in so short a time. I fear we have to hear sad accounts of damage done in various places . . .

[In the margin]. July 13th. I attended the Quarter Sessions at Chesterfield when it appeared that the demand upon the county for the next quarter for the repair of "Bridges" injured by this flood was no less a sum than £7,000 – and the whole sum required for Bridge repairs was no less than £810,000!!! Six Bridges on the Amber swept away!

July 27th, 1830. Calke.

. . . On this day it is the purpose of my dear wife and myself to dedicate in Baptism to the Lord Jesus Christ our dear infant "Isabel Jane", a solemn and interesting ceremony . . . But a year ago and we attended our dear little Henrietta to the Font – and a few weeks afterwards it pleased God to take her to himself – and now in 12 short months we are called upon to perform the same office for our present Babe . . .

August 23rd, 1830. Mendham.

On Saturday afternoon our dear boy John was seized with violent Head-ache accompanied by almost incessant vomiting. This continued thro' the greater part of the night. Fever came on – Calomel, etc, were administered, but without any good effect. Throughout the whole of yesterday (Sunday) he was languid

The Old Vicarage, Mendham.
Photographed by Colin Kitching in 1994.

and drowsy. Twice we sent for the medical attendant – but the stomach rejected his medicine. An Enema was tried, but did not produce the desired effect. About 10 o'clock last night we thought him so unwell that we sent again for the apothecary.

He fell into a tolerably composed sleep. I persuaded my dear wife to go to bed, and untill 2 o'clock I sat up and watched by his Bed-side . . . About 2 o'clock I warmed some gruel for him and gave it to him, and it remained upon his stomach. He fell into a nice sleep and I dozed in the armed chair . . . About 6 o'clock I was awoken by our dear Child suffering from a severe relapse . . . I was grieved to see it, but was rather encouraged by observing that he was more peevish and that his moans proceeded more from his feeling cross and uncomfortable than from any actual pain. I got up and we sent for the medical man who, when he came, said he hoped he was better, but untill the stoppage internally had been removed he could not pronounce him satisfactorily so.

I retired to my room to wash and dress. During that time a happy change took place. The obstruction was relieved, and from that hour a rapid improvement has taken place, and at this moment my beloved Child is prattling by my side – as if nothing had occurred . . .

[Most of the months of September and October were spent at Southwold. The family were back at Calke by October 24th].

November 14th, 1830. Calke. Sunday.

Our dear boy John Harpur, now within a few days of six years old, has under the mercy of God ... a knowledge of religion far beyond his years ... His tenderness of conscience is very peculiar and his remorse, when he has erred, remarkably strong ... This afternoon, as I was sitting by myself in the Dining-room, he came suddenly into the room, much agitated, to tell me that he had been very naughty to his Mamma and had woken his little sister – and had been very angry and spoken very rudely and improperly to his Mamma ...

He left me to beg his Mamma's pardon and request her for forgiveness, having done which he returned to me. I took him upon my knee, and we resumed our conversation. In the course of it I remarked upon his being naturally passionate, and desired that when he was so he did not think as obscure what he did or said. "No, Papa" he said "I will tell you how it is. You know there is Satan – well, Satan does not exactly live in this world, nor in heaven. But he knows and watches all of us, to make us do wrong, and then when I am in a passion, then he comes and whispers in my ear all sorts of wicked and naughty things, and I go and do them" ...

January 21st, 1831. Calke.

... A Fortnight ago my dearest wife left me, with her eldest Brother, to proceed into Suffolk in consequence of a sudden summons to attend her Father who was supposed ... to be not only in imminent danger but without human probability of recovering ... How strange and wonderful it is, then, that at this moment I have to re-count not only that Mr. Whitaker's illness has taken an unexpected and favourable turn, but that so great an improvement has taken place ... that they were able to leave Mendham ... and arrived here, in safety, to dinner by 5 o'clock this day!!!!

February 20th, 1831. Calke.

I have this day witnessed a most melancholy sight. A poor man, a labourer of Ticknall by name "Robt. Dolman", one night last week made an attempt upon his life – first, by wounding himself in the Abdomen with a razor, and then by cutting his throat. In neither case did he, happily, succeed. He was a man of peculiarly industrious habits, having brought up a large family without burden to his parish, and built himself a cottage and rescued a piece of land from the waste for a garden . . .

For the last seven weeks, however, his wife has been very ill and unable to earn a penny. He himself, from some cause or other, had become for a while disabled. On Wednesday last he went to the Vestry to apply for relief. He was not refused, but he was told that The Parish Officer not being there he must come again. Whether this chagrined him, whether he thought his neighbours treated him unkindly, or what were his exact feelings, I know not. But . . . as far as I at present know (for I did not like to ask questions when in his cottage), the next day either when using his razor or chancing to catch his eye upon it, he suddenly took the unhappy resolution there to end all his miseries . . .

Having myself felt what it was to be under the influence of despair I could sympathise with the poor sufferer. I never, never shall forget that night when, in a moment of Agony of mind, I casually cast my eye upon my Razor as it lay upon my Dressing-Table, nor the horrible strength with which "The Tempter" engaged me with the idea "There is a remedy at once that will put an end to all". I had strength given to me immediately to take my razor, knife, Gun and every such weapon and place them where without making noise or disturbance I could not reach them that night . . .

Sunday, March 20th, 1831. Calke.

. . . I went on Wednesday to the Assizes, and only returned at mid-day yesterday. The Grand Jury was not dismissed until nearly five o'clock upon the second day of their sitting – and then I was obliged to adjourn directly to the Bell Inn [in Derby] to meet a party of gentlemen to hold a consultation relative to the intended County meeting to be held upon the subject of Reform on Tuesday next, in Derby. There I was under the absolute necessity of talking nearly the whole time untill 10 o'clock, when I retired to bed weary, feverish and uncomfortable . . .

[Parliamentary reform had been a running sore politically for many years, especially in relation to the franchise and to the distribution of seats in the House of Commons. In the counties of England and Wales the right to vote required, for example, the possession of freehold property with a land tax value of at least 40 shillings a year. In the boroughs the qualifications were often esoteric –

freemen of the borough only, or householders paying the poor rate, or householders not receiving poor relief. The reformers felt passionately that voting rights should be more widely allocated, though they mostly stopped short of the concept of universal adult suffrage.

In regard to the distribution of seats the main problem lay in the absurd population anomalies created by the industrial revolution and the movement of people from the country to the new towns. There were too many MPs representing constituencies (eg, "rotten boroughs") with few voters: on the other hand, rapidly expanding manufacturing towns were grossly under-represented.

In November 1830 the Duke of Wellington's Conservative government resigned and a Liberal (Whig) administration under Lord Grey took over, pledged to act on parliamentary reform. In March 1831 Lord John Russell, one of the most forceful advocates of reform, introduced what came to be known as the first Reform Bill. The meeting of leading Derbyshire Tories Sir George attended at that time was called to consider the Party's attitude to this Bill, which had just passed its second reading. Sir George's views on and anxieties about parliamentary reform are vividly described a little later].

Sunday, March 27th, 1831. Calke.

. . . On Sunday in last week I was confined to the house. In the early part of the week I was obliged to attend a county meeting on the subject of Reform in Parliament, relative to the Bill now before the House upon that important topic . . .

On the day following, as a magistrate I had to investigate the circumstances of a Fire in Appleby [Appleby Magna, Leics.], about ten miles from here, kindled doubtless by the hand of some misguided incendiary. I was not successful in bringing home to the offender the actual perpetration of the crime, altho I have in my own heart but little doubt as to his identity. As it may possibly happen that even in this world the judgement of a righteous Providence may overtake him, I will merely record that the name of the suspected party is "Thomas Measham", a farmer of Appleby . . .

Sunday, April 17th, 1831. Calke.

. . . On Wednesday in the week before last I left Calke, attended by my brother Charles, called at Leicester, it being the time of Sessions, and went into Court for the purpose of having the usual oaths of Office administered to me under the new Commission. This ceremony having been performed, we set forward again and reached Dunstable that evening. On Thursday we arrived in London about one o'clock – remained there during Friday, and on Saturday morning, at 7 o'clock breakfasting, we started for Dover, which place we reached just before dusk. We hastened to 17 Marine Parade, drank tea with my dear sister Selina [Mrs. Selina Badcock], whom we found still up and stirring about.

The following day we spent at Dover. Attended divine service twice at the principal church, dined with Captain Badcock and drank tea with my two elder sisters [Fanny and Louisa] at their house upon Liverpool Terrace. Just before we went to bed we heard that it was probable my dear sister's accouchement would take place in the course of the night ...

On the following morning when my servant came in to call me, he brought me a note, from my sister Louisa, saying that dear Selina's sufferings were happily over, and that she had a nice little girl. This setting our minds at rest, at 7 o'clock we proceeded upon our journey ... The following day was spent in London in the transaction of business I had left uncompleted on Friday. Part of the next morning was also similarly employed, and at 2 o'clock we set out upon our journey homewards ...

Sunday, April 24th, 1831. Calke.

... The most important political event of a domestic nature which has ever occurred since I have been able to think of such things has just taken place. In consequence of two majorities in the House of Commons against the Ministry [Lord Grey's Whig Government] upon the question of Reform, the Ministers thought it necessary to tender their resignation. His Majesty William the 4th did not feel it necessary to accept their offer, but preferred to take the sense of his people upon the Question by the only means in his power. He went down in person on Friday and prorogued Parliament with a view to its immediate Dissolution.

In consequence of this the whole country is very naturally in a state of Agitation and Ferment. One member of the Tory Interest in Derbyshire has signified his intention not to offer himself again. A successor must be looked for. I am in that station which justifies me to offer myself as his successor, were I so inclined – and even if I am not so inclined it is within the reach of probability that I may be solicited to undertake the arduous and, in these days, very hazardous office. Were times more quiet, and my health as strong as that of some people, I should not so much feel the reluctance which now prevails with me . . .

April 28th, 1831. Calke.

I have reason to record that the Lord has heard my Prayer. On Monday I attended the meeting of the most influential persons in the Blue Interest, at Chaddesden. Had the party been unanimous I must have come forward in its support, but the dissension of two or three persons, on account of my having taken a part in favour of Reform at the last County meeting, placed me in that situation that I felt myself imperatively called upon to decline the honour. Thus have I, for the present, been furnished with the means of escaping a situation which I could not envy . . .

June 11th, 1831. Calke.

It has again pleased Almighty God to bring my dear Wife to the hour of trial in child-birth; but a few days more than 12 months have elapsed since the birth of our last dear infant, now by God's mercy alive and healthy. How strange and novel to us, who for many years were almost tempted to fear we should never be blessed with children at all. For several years it pleased God to withhold the precious gift, doubtless for *good* reasons; in a while he gave to us the comfort of our dear boy [John] – then again four years elapsed, and our dear Henrietta was born. In two short months and it pleased God to call her back to himself – within one year and our dear Isabel was given to us, and now a year more and we are looking with anxious hope for another pledge of mutual love!!!

June 22nd, 1831.

It is curious to record, but the appearances, which upon the 10th of this month indicated my dear wife's approaching confinement, all disappeared. She recovered her normal health and was not taken seriously in labour until three o'clock this morning, when her pains became regular, and in proper course. About five o'clock the nurse came to call me up – and I went to see her, a little agitated but upon the whole very comfortable.

[Marginal note] Our dear boy George Harpur was born at 8 o'clock of the morning of June 22nd, and was taken from us by *Him* who gave on the 26th of

June 1838 – he was our finest, strongest child in body and mind, all our hearts could desire.

[*First Reform Bill.* The next extract from Sir George's journal demonstrates his anxieties concerning the failure of the first Reform Bill (1831) to pass through the House of Lords It is difficult for us to-day to appreciate the apprehensions aroused at the time by the process of Parliamentary reform. Britain had so far escaped the revolutionary turmoil which affected continental Europe in varying degrees: but the pressure for reform in the United Kingdom was great enough to create the possibility of insurrection. In particular, the aristocracy and landed gentry were fearful that the long-established order of things might come to a violent end. As will be seen, however, Sir George Crewe was in favour of reform and was critical of those who sought to impede it.

An introduction to the local scene in Derbyshire is necessary. On Saturday, October 8th, 1831, the "Express" stagecoach passed through Derby on its way to Manchester from London, and a crowd waiting in the Cornmarket were told that the Lords had rejected the Bill. Their anger was intense. They insisted that the church bells in Derby should be rung immediately, in mourning. At about 10 pm the crowd attacked the premises of Mr. Bemrose, a printer, where an anti-reform petition had been displayed for signature. They went on to damage the houses of a number of prominent opponents of reform. Finally, a mob attacked and severely damaged Markeaton Hall (the seat of Francis Mundy, MP) and Chaddesden Hall, the home of the Wilmot family.

The next day, Sunday, an intense state of excitement prevailed throughout the town. At 9 am the Mayor held a public meeting to appeal for peace and quiet; it ended in confusion. The mob then demanded the release of three men arrested the previous night. This not being conceded, they marched to the Town Gaol, broke down the doors and freed 23 prisoners.

The crowd then moved on to the County Gaol and attacked it. But the Governor was well prepared and eventually ordered shots to be fired. This dispersed the mob, though not before a young man called Garner had been shot dead (the inquest returned a verdict of justifiable homicide). That evening the crowd re-assembled at the Gaol but the arrival of a troop of Hussars prevented an attack. Instead the demonstrators moved through the town damaging many houses on their way.

On Monday morning, October 10th, there were renewed disturbances. The

Riot Act was read at mid-day and the soldiers ordered to disperse the mob. In doing so they shot and killed a man named John Hickin. Order was restored by a combined force of Hussars, the Radbourne troop of Yeomanry, the Burton-on-Trent Yeomanry, a body of the Derbyshire Militia and a number of special constables.

From all this we can begin to understand the fears so portentously expressed by Sir George.]

Sunday evening, October 9th, 1831.

It is impossible, on a memorable occasion like the present, in a moment pregnant with consequences no human calculation can anticipate, to resist making a slight record of present circumstances.

To-day as I got out of the carriage on my return from Ticknall church I saw my housekeeper standing by the steps, ready to speak to me ... She communicated to me some intelligence that there had been a dreadful riot in Derby last night, that the mob after having demolished windows, etc, in the houses of several residents had proceeded to Chaddesden where they had committed great devastation, and also to Markeaton where they had not only broken windows but proceeded to enter and destroy furniture, etc.

It appears the news of the rejection of the Reform Bill (unwisely as I think) by the Lords reached Derby last night at 7 o'clock. By 8, or soon after, a handbill was circulated by a printer announcing the event. Shortly afterwards the mob collected and proceeded to violence – as remarked before. The blow is struck – the crisis is developed – God only knows in what state of excitement this yesterday quiet kingdom now is.

Monday, October 10th

The tidings this morning are not good; more riots took place last night. The little villa of Harrison, the whitesmith on Little Chester Green, had all its windows and furniture demolished. Poor young Haden, son of Haden the surgeon, was struck on the pit of the stomach by a brick-bat and died shortly afterwards [Haden's death resulted in the conviction and execution of three men]. By 10 o'clock all was quiet tho' attempts were threatened on the County Gaol. No news from London yet.

The same day – 9 o'clock pm

I have received intelligence that the multitude intend this night to pay a visit either to me or to my friend Wilmot at Chaddesden. Be it so, if such is the will of Almighty God. I am very unwilling to make any great preparations for what is called defence – that is to arm myself with defensive weapons. I have no reason to believe that any individual would attack my person, and as for my windows, etc, if any wreaking of vengeance on them would afford satisfactory gratification, they are welcome. To defend the lives of my dear wife and children and the persons of the females in my house is all I would attempt to do.

Tuesday, October 11th, 1831.

I am most thankful to record that we have passed a quiet night. I sat up until ½ past 2 am in our bedroom and I trust employed myself profitably in reading – meditation – prayer.

Friday, October 14th

Most thankful am I to be able to record that the disturbances have not as yet been renewed. The Lord of all mercy has, I trust, heard our poor prayers and spread a spirit of peace amongst the disturbed people.

November 21st. Calke.

I take up my pen this evening to record an awful visitation in our family. One of our household has been taken from us this day. On Saturday morning last I sent my carriage with my sister-in-law and her children to take them home to Breadsall, they having come to attend the christening of our dear infant [George].

As they were in the close carriage my old and faithful coachman, William Shaw, drove the wheelers from the box, and Robert Newhill, second postillion, rode and drove the leaders. Bradbury, my first postillion, went with the carriage instead of the footman.

It appears they got very safe to Breadsall and thence [back] to the Bell Inn at Derby where they baited their horses. They set off from Derby upon their return about a quarter past four o'clock. When within a mile of Chellaston they passed a labourer on the road who had been a long journey on foot and a friend

Breadsall Village, Derbyshire.
Drawn by G. R. Vawser in 1868.

of Shaw's, who he proposed to take up behind – and did so. They pulled up at the Rose and Crown in Chellaston to drop Shaw's friend, who treated him to a glass of ale.

Thence they proceeded to Swarkestone where Shaw's wife lives. There they stopped at the Crewe and Harpur Arms, whilst Shaw ran down to speak to his wife. He soon returned and she was with him. The night being very cold he offered to treat the boys to a glass of brandy and water which they had, and he also took one, but a smaller one. When they came to Melbourne, to the surprise of the men, it being so very contrary to his usual habits, he pulled up at the inn kept by Mrs. Warren, where he called for a quart of ale, of which he drank two glasses himself and gave one to the labourer and one to Robert Newhill. By this time it appeared that he became more talkative than common, being usually a very silent man. This Bradbury observed, but he drove very well until opposite the fishponds in the park where he appeared not to have his usual command over the horses. He turned into the stableyard but in the further end of the gateway he caught the end of the splinter bar against the wall and with some difficulty got his horses right again and drove the carriage to the usual place of halting.

This done he threw down the reins. Bradbury began to take off the horses when he heard something fall. He ran round and found that poor Shaw had fallen upon his left side, first upon the horse's back and thence to the ground. Believing it to be probably in consequence of the liquor he had drunk it was hushed up that night. Yesterday morning at breakfast I was told that Shaw was not well and that he had had a fall in getting off the box. Mr. Child was sent for, who pronounced him in such a favourable state that I thought but little of it.

I enquired again that night and I was told that he was better. But this morning at breakfast my butler told me Shaw was very ill indeed. Immediately that I had finished my breakfast I went to him and the very first glimpse I had of his countenance convinced me he was dying. Mr. Child came and having seen him again assured me that I need not be under the least alarm for there was no present symtom of danger. I confess my heart misgave me when he said what I could not credit after the melancholy testimony of my own eyes.

I had an engagement with a tenant about a mile off and I started about half past eleven to fulfil it. I might be gone about an hour and threequarters. On my return I went up to his room. The moment I saw him I perceived he was on the very acme of his departure. I spoke to him and asked him whether he felt at all worse. His answer, which his poor wife heard by listening to him, was "It is all over with me now".

His poor partner becoming quite frantic I was obliged to move to her and force her to sit down in a chair. I ran downstairs for assistance to his poor wife and ere my footsteps could have reached the bottom of the staircase his spirit had fled from its tenement of clay.

Here is a melancholy tale – poor William – he was as honest, sober, industrious, civil a man as ever entered a house. What could have possessed him to take such an unusual quantity of drink that evening God only knows. But I cannot think otherwise than that he was in a degree not master of his proper senses. I grieve I did not visit him yesterday and I very much fear I was guilty of a neglect of my duty in not having so done, but I was so entirely deceived as to his real state that knowing him to be a very reserved and shy man I thought I would not intrude myself upon him – and when I did go to him it was too late to talk much with him.

November 24th, 1831.

I am just returned from superintending the arrangements for poor William Shaw's funeral and have had the pleasure of assisting in paying every possible respect to the remains of my faithful servant.

November 30th

Only one week has elapsed and I have to record a second disaster which was in its first appearance more frightful than that which caused the death of poor Shaw. On Monday afternoon, about half past four o'clock, my dear wife came to tell me that William Pegg, of Calke, who has for some time been insane, had attacked Mr. Child [the surgeon] with a knife and wounded him very severely. At first I could make but little of the report so I sent my butler to make further enquiries. He came back and gave me such a frightful account as urged me to take my hat and proceed to the village of Calke, where Mr. Child lay at my gardener's house, with all possible expedition.

I found him most dreadfully wounded in the face – such a gash I have never before witnessed – and was told that he had also a worse wound in the side or rather across the right breast. Mrs. Child was there, of course, in the greatest distress altho' she bore up wonderfully and appeared quite composed. The house was crowded with persons – Pegg's two sisters were there half-frantic with what their brother had done and the state of their poor mother who appeared to be never likely to recover. By degrees I succeeded in calming them.

I sent four strong men to see that Pegg was put under proper restraint, a medical attendant to his poor mother – and returned home to make arrangements for Mr. Child being taken home in our carriage.

Really the whole appeared like a dream when it was all over, and I could scarcely rest all night from the perpetual recurrence of the scene of distress of which I had been a witness! Oh! how thankful ought we to be that murder was not actually committed!!! In addition to the blows or cuts I have alluded to there were several more upon the head. The collar of the coat was cut thro' in several places, the waistcoat also in two places. So narrow an escape is seldom met with – I have reason to think that Mr. Child had aggravated him in the first instance and they had had a scuffle which terminated in his pulling out his knife and making use of it, as it appears he afterwards stated himself, in his own defence.

December 12, 1831.

To-day may be a memorable day. This evening will be presented by the Govt. to the House of Commons the new Reform Bill; humanly speaking, one can hardly expect it to be attended with more success than was the former one because unless it be very materially altered in many parts the opposing party will persevere in their hostility and if it be in the opinion of the multitude at all robbed of what in their eyes formed its principal honours, the tumult will be as great as has been the tumult in its favour.

Vain, vain is the help of man – I see no way to turn in which human skill or human wisdom can or will be of much avail. I think I never remember any question of like importance which was argued in both Houses with less of proper regard to the merits of the question than was the Reform Bill. With the exception of an isolated speech here and there the whole debate was one continued tirade between two violent parties who like two savage mastiffs were more engaged in snarling and growling at each other than in regarding the bone that lay between them. Happy are they if they don't find that, whilst they were quarrelling, a little cur, whom they had treated with contempt, has run off with it.

December 15th

Here is a beautiful day to be out of doors in exercise. The fox hounds meet about two miles from hence and in other and better times I should have felt inclined to have taken a gallop.

December 20th

I take up my pen now to advert to the all-engrossing topic which for so long a period has occupied the minds of all ranks and classes of society – the Reform Bill. Parliament assembled upon the 6th of this month and on Saturday last the 2nd reading [in the House of Commons] of the Reform Bill was carried by a majority of 162.

Parliament is adjourned – and it remains, if it pleases God to spare our lives until the opening of another year, that the issues of the struggle will be seen. 1831 has been an eventful year – but it may be less so than 1832, of which it is the forerunner. Should the Bill be again thrown out [ie, by the Lords] Heaven only knows what the awful consequences may be. Should it be carried, its effects, whether good or evil, must be such as no measure has produced for many, many long years.

April 15th, 1832.

I find by the report of the public prints this morning arrived that the 2nd reading [in the House of Lords] of the tedious Reform Bill was carried yesterday morning at 7 o'clock by a majority of 9 – being Sunday, of course. I cannot feel otherwise than thankful that such a result should have taken place. I should hope that our county town, Derby, is consequently in a state of quiescence, comparative at least to what it would have been had the opposite result taken place.

May 10th. Calke Abbey.

Yesterday morning at a quarter past 5 o'clock I set off from Mendham, breakfasted at Bury St. Edmunds, dined at Thrapston and reached Leicester when the clock was upon the stroke of nine. I left Leicester at 6 o'clock this morning and reached this place at 20 mins. before 9.

In consequence of my being engaged upon the journey all day yesterday, and not asking for the newspapers at Leicester, I did not hear the important political event which has taken place. It appears Lord Lyndhurst made a motion upon the Reform Bill, as I am told, to this effect of alteration – that they should begin by enfranchising the new places before they disenfranchise the old ones. This he proposed without any wish to throw out the Bill altogether but as a necessary step, in his opinion, whereby to make it palatable to all parties.

Lord Grey, however, was of the opinion that this went to neutralize his measure so much as to amount to the destruction of his intentions. He therefore put off the further consideration of the Bill until Thursday – this day – and he and the Lord Chancellor immediately set off to the King at Windsor. I met Mr. Jenney in the Park, who told me this much.

When I came back to the stable I heard thro' Mr. Draper (Farrier) that the Mail had brought intelligence this morning that ministers had all resigned. Here is then arrived at last the frightful, awful crisis – what is to follow God alone knows – doubtless it will be that which seems best to his unerring wisdom.

May 16th, 1832. Mendham.

It is impossible not to feel tempted to keep up some record of these eventful times. If not to myself, at least to those who survive me (should this book fall into the hands of the curious) it will be amusing to know how people felt in what will then be termed those awful, those eventful times.

This morning a new report has reached us – that the Duke of Wellington has failed in procuring a union of his own party, in forming a ministry, and that the King has sent for Lord Grey, as is supposed to request him to stay in office. This may, under the blessing of God, have one good effect, that of promoting peace and preventing tumult.

[Following the resignation of Lord Grey's Whig administration King William IV invited the Duke of Wellington to form a government. He failed, and the King was obliged to call on Lord Grey to resume office, it being understood that – if necessary – sufficient peers wold be created to ensure the passing of the Reform Bill through the House of Lords. In fact the Bill received the Royal Assent in June.

Among other measures the new Act provided for (i) the redistribution of 143 parliamentary seats, 44 of which went to expanding industrial towns and to London, and (ii) standardised and extended franchise qualifications which, in the boroughs, included householders paying rent of at least £10 a year and, in the counties, brought in a new range of freeholders, leaseholders and tenants.

The Reform Act of 1832 damped down much of the agitation which had precipitated it. But the more radical reformers were far from satisfied with legislation which, though it provided for a better distribution of seats, increased the electorate in England and Wales only from some 435,000 to 700,000. Sir George refers to the continued pressure for further parliamentary reform in his entry for May 17th 1833.]

May 27th, Sunday. Calke Abbey.

On Thursday morning last we started – my dear wife, myself and children – from the sweet abode of my dear Father-in-law upon our return to this our proper home. The morning was a May morning, gay and bright. The nightingale, the thrush, the lark were sweetly chanting their simple praises to the Lord of all, and every bush had its songster of inferior skill, twittering its little carol in their same humble offering.

Fond as I am of that spot, I was grieved at the moment to depart from it, but under any circumstances the parting must be painful. The precarious state of Mr. Whitaker's health renders it but too probable that we have visited him for the last time, and my poor wife could but feel that on that morning, perhaps, she was parting from her Father for ever in this world.

June 9th, 1832. Calke Abbey.

On Friday morning in last week I started from Calke with my Brother Charles for London, having some business to transact there, and a wish, if possible, to go before my dear wife would require my undivided and due attention [she was pregnant again]. We left Calke at 5 o'clock am and arrived in London to a late dinner at past 7 pm. On Saturday I went to the Exhibition [at] Somerset House, it lying in my route to the city – the very worst exhibition I ever yet saw.

At 7 o'clock we started for Shooters Hill on a visit to my dear Sisters Fanny and Louisa, who were delighted at our unexpected arrival. On Sunday morning I walked to Eltham Church. In the evening we, with my dear Sisters, attended Mr. Shepperd's Chapel at Blackheath, which latter was a great comfort in a Sabbath attended with more Bustle than I like or am accustomed to. On Monday morning we returned to town to Breakfast.

And now I must detail one of the most singular occurrences I have met with or may meet with in the course of my life of which I would wish and also feel it necessary to keep some record. In the morning whilst at breakfast I perceived an Advertisement in the Morning Post, addressed to the benevolent, purporting to come from a young Lady of a good Family who was entitled to some property upon her coming of age, and who upon that wished to borrow the sum of One Hundred Pounds. Being then at Craig's Court, no great distance from the place of reference – No. 9, Barton Street, Westminster – I thought, and indeed felt an almost irresistible impulse, to go there.

I knocked at the door – which was opened by a female servant of the most homely and not of the most cleanly description, who showed me into a sort of drawing-room on the 2nd floor. Presently a young lady, apparently about 19, came to me, to whom I announced myself as a person come in consequence of the advertisement. She requested me to walk up one Pair of Stairs higher. I did so, where I found another lady, a sister as I afterwards discovered, about 23 years of age, I should think. We entered upon the subject of my visit, which was with much artlessness and nervous timidity detailed by the young lady I had first seen.

It appeared that they were persons of good – nay high – connection who had seen better days but had become reduced until gradually they had wanted the necessaries of life. Their Father too was confined to his bed with erysipelas in his left foot and ancle.

It appeared that under the will of their grandfather each of these children was entitled to about £220 in Irish Funded Property. The two eldest had received theirs, and upon the share of the elder sisters they had been living until it was all spent. They had pledged everything which could make money. In these desperate circumstances this girl had placed the advertisement in the Paper with the affectionate wish, if possible, to procure a loan on her inheritance to appropriate to the present relief of her Father and Mother, Sister and two Brothers. No money-lender would advance it because she could give no security. If she died before the age of 21 years her share would be divided between the surviving brothers and sisters.

Knowing alas! how wicked this world is and how frequently such applications are made by rank imposters I sifted all matters as deeply as I could, but there appeared to be nothing but a plain, unvarnished statement in which it was without reserve tho' not without shame that the eldest daughter told me the chief of their then distress had been brought on by the folly and extravagance of their parents in early life.

I was much delighted to hear these two excellent young women speak as they did on this topic. So far from upbraiding their parents even in the slightest degree they seemed only to feel that it was their duty, as it evidently was their inclination, to spend all they proposed to support their parents in their declining years.

I enquired of the youngest, whose name is Sarah, what she meant to do with the money. She said she and her sister would try to keep a school, having been well-educated, and do what they could for their parents. I said to her: "My good girl, I admire and respect your filial affection and industrious intentions, but you will also perhaps want the money more than you do now". To which she replied, with that warmth so incidental to the Irish character, "Oh! but Sir! I *would* never want it more than I do now – my Father and Mother are living, they are sick and helpless and starving, and when it pleases God to take them from us we can work for our bread and do without the money".

I listened to a long, a very interesting conversation which terminated by my persuading them at any rate to take time to consider the matter, and by tending my advice that as they had so many wealthy friends and relatives in Dublin they should consider whether she had not better, if possible, borrow $1/2$ the sum she proposed and all take their immediate depature for Dublin. I left them, promising if I could to return the next day.

This, however, I was unable to accomplish. On Wednesday I attended his Majesty's Levee, having never had opportunity heretofore of being presented to him. As soon as I had rid myself of my court trappings I took a Hackney coach and proceeded to Barton Street. There I saw the same Parties, with the addition of the Father and two nice boys – one about 15, the other 11 or 12. After many warm-hearted expressions on his part, and a further detail of his history and circumstances, he told me they had determined to take my advice and, if possible, to borrow the money which he required immediately to go back to Dublin.

I applauded his resolution. We then entered upon a desultory conversation in which I had opportunity of enquiring into the character and disposition of the family. What the results of my remarks were I need not record – suffice it to say that I was so convinced that I trust to the credibility of their tale that I determined I would grant them the assistance they required – at least in the manner and to the extent which I proposed. I told them I would call again the following morning.

They were all profuse of their thanks at the interest I had taken in them all, and all shed tears of joy – and before I was aware of it, however annoying and unfashionable, I saw the dewdrop on my sleeve which had trickled from my own eye.

On the following morning I procured £60 in Bank of England notes and took it to them. I received a paper acknowledging the debt from them – and gave them one on my part.

The main difficulty throughout was my wish to remain in concealment as to who or what I was. With this in view, and I mention it here in case anything should occur to me or to them, that for the purpose of identifying the transaction I sealed both the papers they gave me with a little Antique which I wear on my Purse, and dated London 7th of June 1832 – which in case any enquiry should be made, will enable any of my family to identify the papers if presented to them.

The Papers I received from Mr. George Sate, for that was the gentleman's name, are in my "Escritoire" and will be found in the little drawer marked with the letter S. Some people will say, why surely you are not fool enough to think you will ever hear of them or see your money again!!! I am fool enough to think the first certain, the next probable. My own belief is that the Lord, who never ceased to have compassion on the afflicted, seeing the pure intentions of that affectionate child for her suffering Parents directed my footsteps to that House to be in his hands the instrument whereby she should be enabled to accomplish her pious purposes.

I heard from their own lips their conviction that it was the hand of God above and his Spirit which had sent and administered the relief to their necessities, and I have every reason to believe that under God's blessing this event has produced a deep religious impression upon their minds which will never be forgotten.

I learnt that they had received no other answer to their advertisement, either by letter or personal application. My heart was too full to remain long with

Calke Abbey. South East View.
Drawn by G. R. Vawser in 1868.

them on this occasion and I hastily ran downstairs, my heart almost trembling when I heard their invocations for the blessings of God on me and mind. Oh! what a delightful day was this.

July 4th, 1832. Calke Abbey.

I commence this new Journal under circumstances rather peculiar. It is within a quarter of the hour of midnight. I am sitting in the Library and on the sofa lies our medical attendant, Mr. Godwin, of Derby, taking a little repose, such as his laborious profession renders very needful. My dearest wife is suffering the throes of that Pain which was entailed upon her sex at the hour of Child-birth, in consequence of the lamentable fall of our first Parent. Thank God, therefore, I am told all is going on as it should do: this is a very great blessing and call for our thankfulness and praise to Him whose mercy has brought her to this hour and whose grace and help alone can carry her thro' her perils . . .

In public affairs of this Kingdom this is an hour of great and severe trial. We are assailed by threatenings of violence and tumult. We are involved in many and great national difficulties and we are surrounded on all sides with that awful scourge "The Cholera", which silently but fatally creeps to and fro, here and there, as tho' its deadly poison would tinge the whole face of the country during its stay amongst us . . .

July 5th, 10 mins past 1 o'clock.

I had written thus far when there came a knock at the door. Mr. Godwin peeped in and said, I am only just come to tell you there is a little boy [Evelyn], and Lady Crewe is very comfortable. As soon as he had closed the door I fell down on my knees before my blessed Saviour and poured out my full – and I think I may say – my grateful thanks for this additional mercy.

July 8th. Sunday.

I have just been to Ticknall Church – it is the Wake Sunday and I grieve to say there was not more than one third of the usually small congregation. The morning was rather damp and I suppose the men were engaged in drinking and the women unwilling to run any risk of injuring their new gowns, or putting hair out of curl before this evening.

Mr. Hill gave us a very good sermon on this text – "This is the victory that overcometh the world, even from Faith". Some parts of the discourse were well suited to the Wake folk, but unhappily this good intention was frustrated for they were not there to hear it. Oh! how I do wish we had a resident minister and one of an active and calm character at Ticknall. I much fear Vice and Irreligions are making rapid strides at that place.

9 o'clock pm

Owing to an attack of Inflammatory Action upon the Trachea I have not now for the 3rd Sunday been able to read a Sermon to my family on Sunday evening, according to my general custom. I hope however, by God's blessing, that I shall by Sunday next be enabled to resume what was to me one of the most delightful of all occupations, that of communing with my Household upon the things which concern our everlasting happiness . . .

July 10th

I resume my pen with a heavy heart. I had my fears this morning when I first went to see my dear Wife and her baby that the latter was not quite so well as it should be and my dear sister-in-law Whitaker has just been with me to say my dear Wife is very anxious about the little darling – I could not but think this morning that there was something very like the symptoms of the indisposition which took from us our dear little Henrietta. My heart is more full than admits of expression . . .

4 o'clock pm

I have been endeavouring to take a walk hoping to compose my mind, but the day is sultry with a warm wind from the south, which is very relaxing, and from agitation of business yesterday and anxiety of feeling to-day I have been attacked by a neuralgic pain in the muscles of my left leg just below the front of the knee, and was obliged to come into the house, almost doubtful whether I could reach it. Our dear little babe was put into a warm bath about nine o'clock, and at first seemed to be much relieved thereby – and thank God he certainly looks somewhat better in appearance . . .

July 11th, Tuesday.

I have indeed to record the mercies of the Lord. Yesterday, after I penned the remarks in this Journal, our dear Infant still appeared very ill. He was put in a warm bath, which appeared to relieve him, and the spasmodic affection appeared less violent. Towards the afternoon he showed a disposition to feed and took his mother's milk cheerfully and with appetite. Towards evening the spasm appeared altogether to subside and this morning when I went into my dear wife's room I had the inexpressible pleasure to find both my dear wife and child had passed a very comfortable night. I cannot record my feelings now, as I am obliged to go to the magistrates meeting at Swarkestone, but hope I shall have leisure so to do when I return.

July 13th

Yesterday being a fine day we made a party to work in the Hayfield – Major and Miss Smyth, John and myself. A very delightful day we had, working very hard. We got up 10 or 12 loads yesterday in very nice order, and thankful we ought to be – for in the course of the evening it began to rain, and by eleven o'clock it rained in torrents. It appears that there has been more rain since that and the clouds, altho' breaking, are very heavy. I fear the weight of the storm will do some injury amongst the corn . . .

The newspapers of last night give dreadful accounts of the Cholera in many parts of England. In London it appears to have broke out afresh, in Liverpool it is very bad, and in York so rife that the Assizes have been postponed. When I have heard persons joke and laugh, as I have done, about that awful complaint, when I saw so many assertions in the public prints ridiculing all idea of fear, and even stating that there was no cause for it, altogether denying that it was the judgement of divine vengeance upon a guilty nation, I have often trembled in anticipation that it must and would return with increased violence . . .

10 o'clock

I have the happiness this morning to find my dear wife and children quite comfortable.

July 14th. Saturday.

It is awful to look at the State of England at this present moment. Visited with a heavy scourge in pestilence, equally visited with the Plague of Internal commotion, Violent Faction & etc, & etc. A House divided against itself cannot stand long, it is impossible. Well – we must wait patiently the will of the Lord . . .

July 15th, Sunday – St. Swithin's Day.

This morning I was awake by the most brilliant of glorious sunrise, but it is the day dedicated to the watery saint and already (10 o'clock) it is cloudy and the wind blows hollow, and there are symptoms of more rain. We ought to be thankful that we have a fresh invigorating breeze instead of the close and heavy atmosphere of the two preceding days. I rode round my farm last night; many indeed most of the crops are much improved by the rain, particularly the Turnips and Wheat. We may believe it is well for us we are not left to the folly of our own choice with regard to weather . . .

July 16th

Nearly a week ago I was in great distress upon account of the illness of my dear infant. The Lord however was merciful, he heard my prayer, he vouchsafed his blessing upon the means used for recovery, and the child now appears altogether thriving and comfortable . . .

July 24th

Yesterday was a lovely day. In the morning I was engaged with my agent. About 1 o'clock I went to the Hay-field where Major Smyth and I worked until ¹/₂ past 7 o'clk pm, when we came home comfortably tired. When I was in the field I could not but contrast the peace and content of the scene before me with the confusion and dissatisfaction which unhappily prevail in many parts of England, owing to the excitement stirred by wicked and designing men who, under cover of proclaiming their country's rights, have no real object at heart but the love of notoriety and the gratification of their own personal vanity. And I could not but see the cause of all this Sin, indwelling innate corruption, the curse which prevails over everything here below. When I came home, I took up the newspapers and much shocked was I at the dreadful account of the cholera, which appears now to be spreading with frightful rapidity over the whole face of the country. In God do I put my trust, let me never be confounded.

How strange it is to see the papers full of accounts of Routs and Splendid Parties, Races and Water-Fetes and every species of expensive gaiety, as if they would show how determined they are to bid defiance, even to the wrath of the most high God . . .

July 25th

It is impossible in these awful times not to feel anxious to keep some memorial of passing events, so fearfully interesting are they. The newspapers of last evening's post give a dreadful account of the rapid increase of the cholera. It has returned to London, with tenfold violence, and is now become quite a pestilence. It is no longer confined to the dwellings of the poor. Several persons of the middle class of life have now been attacked and have fallen victim to the ravages. And the day before yesterday Mrs. Robert Smith, daughter-in-law of Lord Carrington died after only 8 hours indisposition . . .

July 29th

I am just returned from Calke Chapel where I have been attending Divine

Calke Chapel (Church).
Drawn by G. R. Vawser in 1868.

Service. My dear wife accompanied me, to return thanks for her safe delivery from the great pain and perils of childbirth. This was the 4th time in 3 years to her who was deemed by her friends and thought herself likely never to have any children at all. So wonderful are the ways of providence . . .

August 2nd

I am going this morning, by God's blessing and permission, to Derby to attend at the Assizes upon the Grand Jury. This is one of the painful offices which I feel inclined to shrink from, and should do, were it not that a sense of duty kept me to my post.

August 3rd, 1832. Friday.

We were yesterday in the Grand Jury Room until after 6 o'clock. At 7 we went to dine with the Judge, Mr. Justice Parke, senior. I returned home but very late, 1/2 past 11 o'clock . . . One of the trials which formed part of the business in the criminal court at these Assizes . . . [is] worthy of record. It was the trial of Robert McCracken, a stone-mason by trade, for the murder of his wife by administering poison to her. The evidence against McCracken was very strong circumstantial evidence – that the poor woman died from poison, and that the poison was "arsenic", there could be no doubt, and that the poison was administered with the Intention of her death, by her Husband, appeared as strong as mere circumstantial evidence could make it. Still there was no direct evidence to prove that his was the hand which prepared the poisoned draught, and on this doubt, of which they naturally and properly wished to give the accused the benefit, I should imagine the Jury founded their verdict of "Not Guilty".

August 16th

Yesterday was a beautiful Harvest day. But to-day is showery and promises to be very wet. I cannot but hope that the Thunder-storm and the change of weather may be in the end beneficial to the general health of the country. The Cholera, it appears by the newspaper of yesterday, has broke out again in the town of Newcastle-upon-Tyne, one of the places where it first showed itself, as it appears with an increased violence, being more rapidly fatal than it was the first time. And now it has attacked persons generally in the higher grade in life than before, as tho' it were the will of God that all classes in their turn should undergo the heavy scourge . . . I had a long conversation last night with a gentle-man, a member of the Stock Exchange, who is now upon a visit to me, relative to the state of the country at large but more especially to the state of the Metropolis. His account of the general distress, the stagnation of business and universal want of confidence, is most awful . . .

August 25th, 1832

Yesterday I went from home, accompanied by my brother Charles, to Red Hill, 3 miles beyond Nottingham, to meet a Drover of Scotch Cattle. I purchased 20 Polled Galloways at 10 guineas each and 20 Ayrshire Heifers at the same price per head.

August 28th, Tuesday

We have a melancholy topic for remark this morning. It has rained incessantly and during the greater part heavily, for the last sixteen hours – I believe without interruption. The quantity of rain will be sufficient to injure the corn very materially, particularly the Barleys, which are cut and have been down some days – and even that which is not cut will be laid by the very heavy rain.

September 9th, Sunday.

Here is arrived the thirteenth anniversary of my Wedding-day – a day of such importance as an epoch in my wordly life that it is impossible to meet it without a strong excitement of various and somewhat conflicting feelings. I have in every return of this day experienced and in very many extended the sensations which accompanied it. It is a day much to be remembered by me and my dear wife as one on which it pleased God to accomplish and bring to pass that of which mankind almost despaired – and it is a day much to be remembered by me, as one which landed me safe from the tempestuous tossing of a troublesome and sinful world, on whose billows I had been cast without a pilot, at least of this world's friends. Where I have neglected to keep close to my heavenly guide and consequently have well nigh been swallowed up in the depths of sin and misery. When I look back and consider the state of wretchedness from which it pleased God to snatch me – when I reflect upon the promises and vows I then made in full joy of a thankful heart and compared the actual course of my life for the last thirteen years, therewith I am overwhelmed with conscious guilt and deep convictions of my base ingratitude.

September 10th

I was so overcome with my neuralgic pain last night that I was obliged to retire to my bed at an early hour. Thank God, the attack was not nearly so severe as I have at former times experienced. I slept uncomfortably and the Paroxysm did not abate, but came also in the other leg, which had not before been affected. After I got up this morning I felt somewhat relieved and, altho in pain, I have been able to sit quietly in my own room and read . . .

September 12th, 1832

Yesterday I was engaged the whole morning at Swarkestone in investigation of a case of brutal assault by an old man, 70 years of age, upon two little girls – one of the age of 9 years. The capital offence will not be proved and perhaps was never committed, but the assault is a grievous one and will, if he be found guilty, I think be visited with a justly heavy punishment.

Swarkestone Bridge, Derbyshire.
Drawn by Vawser in 1868.

September 16th, Sunday

Yesterday my dear wife and I went to dine at Donnington Park with the Marquis of Hastings. Everything was splendid, in keeping with his rank. To me, as unaccustomed as I have been of late to such intercourse, the splendour was dazzling, and the princely magnificence – whilst it pleased the eye – brought a sensation of heaviness upon the Heart, more particularly in these times of trouble and general distress. Lady Hastings (Baroness de Ruthyn) is a very pleasing, unaffected person, with much in her disposition to attract admiration – and considering the frightful eminence of temptation in which she is placed so young, is a delightful contrast to the artful, studied elegance of the age . . .

On Friday last, whilst my dear wife and I were preparing for bed, in a moment there came, about 11 o'clock, a speale of wind accompanied by tremendous rain and something which was, altho we did not identify it clearly as such, a clap of thunder – it lasted for about 10 minutes, and barely that, and then all was hushed and quiet as before . . .

It appears that during this storm, remarkable for its extreme violence . . . the Rev. Mr. Tunnicliff, incumbent of Hartshorne in this neighbourhood, and a friend of his Mr. Wattington, of the same place, were returning home from

Packington ... The storm came on just as they were within a mile of the Wooden Box, upon the Ashby road (they were travelling in Mr. Tunnicliff's one Horse Phaeton). The flash of lightning and the violence of the storm frightened the Horse and he ran furiously away. Mr. Wattington got out of the carriage, and altho he had a severe shock in his fall, which cut his face deeply, was not materially hurt. Mr. Tunnicliff was carried forward – whether the carriage was overturned or whether he attempted to jump out, or whether he was thrown out, it does not appear that anyone can say.

He was found in the road, at the bottom of the hill, with his skull fractured in two places ... He lingered untill somewhere between three and five, when he expired.

Mr. Tunnicliff was a widower with one Son – grown up. He lost his wife 2 or 3 years ago – she died from the effects of a cancer, was a great sufferer, but I believe was latterly a very decided Christian and died very happily, leaving a good warning to her sorrowing husband to seek the Lord Jesus diligently and to serve him faithfully as a zealous Minister. I am told to-day that he had just re-fitted up the Parsonage and prepared it for a second wife, being engaged to ... a widowed daughter of Mr. Hassall, Senr, of Hartshorne, a Mrs. Deverill, of Smisby.

September 21st, 1832

Yesterday was the day fixed for my brother Edmund's marriage, and a beautiful day it was. On the previous evening Miss Wheldon accompanied me to "Bury Hill" [near Mansfield, Notts.], the seat of Mrs. Walker, where we met a pleasant family party and were introduced for the first time to General Need, the father of the bride elect, and Colonel Need, her uncle. The Evening passed off very agreeably.

On the following morning I was roused early by the maidservant coming to light my fire ... About $1/2$ past nine we started for Fountain Dale [the home of General Need and the bridge, $1^1/2$ miles north west of Blidworth], 4 carriages in number. There arrived, we found a large number, in addition, assembled. At $1/2$ past 10 we started again – in all ten carriages – for Blidworth, a small country village in the centre of the once famous "Sherwood Forest". The Church is ancient, and simple in its structure. There the ceremony, both religious and civil, which united my dear Brother Edmund to Miss Caroline Need, was performed with great solemnity not too much "piety", by Mr. Darnall, the curate – I suppose – perhaps the incumbent Blidworth.

I was standing in the rear of the company assembled round the Altar, and whilst waiting for some little preliminaries, such as presenting the Licence, etc, etc, I could but remark the pictorial beauty of the group, which had been casually arranged with greater elegance than perhaps could have been accomplished by any contrivance of design.

We returned to "Fountain Dale" where about 34 or 35 sat down to breakfast. About 2 o'clock the Bride and Bridegroom started [on their journey] to the Isle of Wight – and immediately afterwards Miss Wheldon and I took our departure for home, where we arrived – by God's blessing – in safety at six o'clock and found a few friends waiting to dine with us in celebration of the wedding day: Mr. and Mrs. Jenney, 2 sons and 2 daughters, Mr. and Mrs. Wright Whitaker [brother and sister-in-law], Rev. and Mrs. Witt, Major and Miss Amelia Smyth, and Mr. William Smith, Senr. of Swarkestone. As I enjoy a wedding in the country, so naturally gay and so hearty in its innocent mirth, I could but be pleased with one of the prettiest and best arranged weddings I ever was present at. It reminded me forcibly of the happy day which united me to my dearest Jane 13 years ago.

September 26th. Chatsworth.

This evening finds me for the first time in my life in a Palace. I say a Palace for altho the Noble owner is not a Prince the style of the House is princely, and more so, I suspect than would be found in the mansion of many ones born to that high and mighty title.

Unaccustomed as I am to mix with the world it was impossible for me not to experience a considerable degree of awkwardness – yes, downright awkwardness, that is the right word – in finding myself suddenly immersed in the vortex of that world of which I hear much but know so little. It is so late to-night that I cannot go very far in my description. Suffice it to say my first sensation on entering the grounds was a sort of rustic astonishment at the magnificence of all around me. On entering the splendid room allotted to me, in which I am now writing, the splendour of the Palace was oppressive to me – oppressive from a combination of feelings which I have not at this moment leisure to analyze, much less to describe.

September 27th

I retired last night to my splendid couch, tired but not sleepy. But after a while the pleasing torpor came over me and I slept soundly and have risen refreshed and have lost the head-ache which the noise of a Public Dinner had afflicted me with. I rose about ¼ before 8, later than I could wish, but I was not in bed untill near one o'clock. I am now a little relieved from the variety of feelings which yesterday overwhelmed me and am more at liberty to proceed with the record of my feelings or observations.

Yesterday was the annual meeting of the Scarsdale and High Peak Agricultural Society. The attendance was tolerably numerous. The show of cattle but moderate, indeed some were positively bad. His Grace of Devonshire and several friends showed themselves in the Field. Lord Newburgh, accompanied by Lord Adolphus Fitzclarence, Mr. Western the well-known agriculturist of Essex, and General Renoldson or Rennison or some such name, for I could not catch it correct.

At 3 o'clock we sat down to dinner [at an inn in Bakewell], to the number of about forty five . . . The dinner passed off very well, with the exception of one poor man who seemed determined to drink more than was right, inasmuch as he would have a bottle of wine to himself. We had no touch upon politics, happily, as Bakewell is a warm place in that respect. At 6 o'clock Mr. Ashby took a seat in my carriage and we drove to this place [ie Chatsworth]. We sat down to dinner, about 24 persons – who they all were I am not clear . . .

September 28th. Chatsworth.

About 9 o'clock, an hour which here is called early, I with difficulty found my way out of the house into the garden – journey I should not have accomplished with a right termination but for the kind assistance of a Lady's maid casually crossing the court – who, perceiving me to be a stranger, with all the quickness and kindness which characterizes the sex, not only showed me the way but opened the door for me.

I wandered, for an hour and a half, in the Gardens, which are a beautiful and elegant appendage to this princely mansion. The morning was warm as a day in June. The sun had dispersed the mist, somewhere it hung on the distant mountains' brow. I think I never saw a more magnificent or a more lovely scene. The "location", as an American would say of this place, is extraordinarily beautiful. A Palace situate in the midst of wild scenery, where Nature revels in her own beauty, unfettered by art and unspoilt by caprice, and presents a scene of singular beauty, to estimate which would require the careful study of many days. I shall have a great deal to do in a short time, therefore must lay aside my pen for the present, in order that I may lose no part of this lovely day.

2 o'clock

I have been walking with my friend Beaumont through the House, viewing the improvements and additions – when complete it will be without doubt one of the very finest and most magnificent places in the Kingdom – of the kind – perhaps in the world – and of which I can say no more or less than that it is only too large and too magnificent for any one man.

12 at night

Specimen of the hours kept here – I am just arrived in my Bed-room!! O Tempora – O Mores! Reform is a goodly cry – Reform!!

September 29th. Calke.

Yesterday morning I left the Temple of Luxury at 11 o'clock to return to my own quiet home – and most thankful I am to record that I found my dear Wife and Children in good health. The relief of the change was great. The Duke was kind enough to wish me to have staid another day and joined a Party of Pleasure which was bound for Buxton. But I declined it, being very anxious to return home. I waited until the Party, in three carriages and four, had started. I hope and believe the little change of air was beneficial to my health and I trust, under God's grace, not injurious to my spiritual interests . . .

October 5th. Mendham.

In how different as well as distant a part of the countryside I this night find myself. I left my sweet home on Tuesday morning, accompanied by my Brother-in-law Wright Whitaker and our two dear boys . . . We had, thank God, a very pleasant journey, with the exception of the latter part, which was to me painful as I had a very sharp attack of my old enemy – which caused me a feverish and disturbed night, last. I am thankful to say that I am better this evening . . . I found my poor Father-in-law looking thinner than when we left him in May last, but considering all things much better than we then ever expected to see him again.

October 12th. Calke Abbey.

I started upon my return to my own dear home on Wednesday morning having as my companions Elizabeth Whitaker and my dear boy John. We reached Bury [St. Edmunds] about mid-day ... We proceeded to Cambridge, where we slept, and the following morning at 9 o'clock we started for home. At Market Harbro I heard that my dear wife had been very ill – which caused the rest of the journey to pass heavily. At Ashby-de-la-Zouch the servant who came to meet me brought a note from my sister-in-law containing the welcome news that my dear Jane was better. On my arrival I found her in bed in a state of very great weakness, and much overcome at the sight of me, as on the Tuesday previous she had entertained fears lest she should never be permitted to see me again.

She had had a bilious head-ache in the preceding week and was, as she thought, nearly recovered from its effects. On Tuesday last, however, at 6.0am she was seized with violent spasmodic Pains in the Bowels, accompanied with dreadful and incessant sickness, symptoms so correspondent with those of the Cholera that she could not but suppose that was her malady. About 11 the violence of the attack yielded to the medicine administered thro the blessing of God ...

October 20th

On Monday, in consequence of my having been from home, business of a variety of kinds had accumulated upon me and I was perplexed – or, to use a more vulgar but more expressive term, quite bothered therewith.

On Tuesday I went to Derby to attend our Quarter Sessions. I went to Mr. and Mrs. Evans at Allestree to dine and sleep. On Wednesday I was in court all day – dined with the Magistrates at the County Tavern, and returned to Allestree to sleep. On Thursday we went into court at 9 o'clock am and had finished business about half past 2. The Lawyers were quarrelsome and we had a stormy debate, once or twice on points of law. I had two or three engagements in Derby and returned home about 1/2 past 5 o'clock.

October 25th

On Wednesday I attended at Derby the adjourned Quarter Sessions, for regulation of the Polling Districts for the Southern Division of this County. To-day I ought to have attended a Rail-Road meeting at Sir G. Beaumont's, but I sent my agent instead of myself. I have not had a day of relaxation for a very long time and the Fox-hounds met at Ingleby Hill, about two miles from here, and I thought I would for once endeavour to invigorate myself by a Gallop with them. The day was beautiful. The Hounds never went a field beyond the wood, but one of them got but a mile or so – the scents bad.

We returned to the house, and after about an hour's running killed a young fox – one, I should think, of at least half a dozen which were on foot at different times. Could I have foreseen that they would remain there all day I should have stayed at home to be present at the marriage of Mary Hough, our head Laundry-maid, to Robert Miles, the eldest son of my Pensioner, Mrs. Miles, at Fressingfield. Oh! if the poor lady who (under the grace of our Lord Jesus Christ) is now, I think, awaiting an eternity of bliss, could but have seen her Robert married from this house, how she would have cried with joy.

My Butler, Mr. Sutton, took the Bride, next followed the Bridegroom with Mary Wilks, the Head-housemaid, and then John Kirby with Mary Dean, the second House-maid, these two being the Bridesmaids, neatly dressed in white, with white Ribbons in their Bonnets of Straw. The men had large nose-gays. My dear wife and her sister had previously walked up to the Church to be present at the wedding. All went off very nicely. At 2 o'clock they sat down to a good dinner prepared for them, to which they were permitted to invite their friends, and to-night they will have a party at Tea. Mary has lived with us 12 or 13 years and Robert had been my Protege for nearly 17 years. I attended his poor Father during a lingering illness of many a year, and was I believe the last person to whom he spoke – and one of the last things he said to me was that now I had promised to be a friend to his children he should die happy and contented … The Bride and Bridegroom have just been upstairs in my study to speak to me. I wish them joy and success with all my heart.

October 27th, 1832

I cannot rest without unburdening my mind altho in doing so am about to record my own folly. I was so pleased with my ride to see the hounds, and have always felt such benefit in the exercise as a relaxation from business, that I determined I would purchase a good steady Hunter such as I could now and then ride with comfort. A dealer told me in the Field that he had several and would come over and shew them to me, as this morning. When I returned home I considered it and thought that if I allowed the man to come over I should be obliged to purchase. So yesterday being a leisure day I rode over with my

Stanton-by-Bridge Rectory, Church and School, Derbyshire.
Painted by Sir George Crewe, c. 1841.

brother Charles to Horninglow, near Burton-on-Trent, and thence to Rolleston, to which place we heard Mr. Lathbury had removed. There I saw several horses, one a grey with which I was very much pleased.

The prices were ruinously high and such as I had never given for my own use in my life. I considered that this man when he begged me to be a customer (for he had filled his stables at a great expense and from the badness of the times found few customers) was entitled to my support in his calling, as a gentleman living in the neighbourhood. After arguing with myself some time and considering what other horses I could part with to reimburse me for the expence of this one I agreed to give him 120 guineas, in money, and a mare valued at 20 guineas, in exchange for this grey mare.

When, however, I returned home I felt very uncomfortable. Some may say, how ridiculous. Very likely – but I had never in my life been guilty before of an act of such extravagance for my own selfish personal gratification and I stood convicted of folly at the bar of my own conscience.

[Marginal note] December 22nd, 1832: The Horse alluded to proved restiff and ungovernable and was consequently returned to the dealer.

November 15th

I steal a moment to make a memorandum of no small importance to me and mine. On Monday the 12th inst. the 3rd son of my old tutor, Dr. Bloxam – the Rev. Andrew Bloxam – came to reside in my family as Tutor to my dear boy John. He is grown too large for the management of women, from the increase of family with which it has pleased God to bless us. My dear wife cannot attend to him and my business as a magistrate and country gentleman is so incessant that I cannot give him that attention which otherwise it would be my duty to do. Mr. Bloxam is well qualified for the task, not only in classical but more particularly in general knowledge. He is a person of unimpeachable morals, of practical piety, of quiet unassuming manner and excellent temper.

December 11th

I had occasion yesterday to go to Radbourne, the seat of E. S. Pole, Esq, to attend the 2nd meeting of our County Rate committee. Thinking the ride would do me good and shake off the bilious feeling which from much confinement to the house I have felt for several days past I mounted my favourite horse "Cupid", of whose beauty, speed and fine temper I had long been justly proud. I found him very fresh, having had but little work of late, but as I wished him to go fast I thought but little of it. As usual he squibbed and jumped and danced about, but in excellent humour. I chanced to miss my way, and by that means fell into a road before unknown to me. This took me into the village of Littleover.

As I was passing up the hill, a man coming rather suddenly out of a house by the Road-side caused "Cupid" to start. He became agitated, as he frequently is when very fresh. I tried to pacify him, but in vain. He bolted up the Hill, nor could I obtain perfect command of him until he had proceeded some distance along the Turn-pike road. I cantered on and thought no more about the matter.

This morning, after breakfast, I set off upon my return home. I found my nag very gay but pleased. We had a good deal of work in some miry lanes which made him a little impatient, but nothing worth mentioning. Still, I could every now and then perceive that all was not right, and the Horse appeared – unusual with him – considerably out of humour. We went on very well, with a few little squibs and jumps, until we came to a lane where I turned down for Tywford, from Findern. There he jumped – what at I cannot tell – bolted down the lane, started afresh at some water passing through a small bridge and soon began apparently to pull with more than usual determination. At length he bolted thro an open gate into a field and tore up the Hill, apparently quite frantic, with his head up; he bid defiance to all my powers to stop him.

I became at first alarmed, but lifting up my heart in silent prayer to God I began to speak to him and, at last, with great difficulty, at the hedge I stopped him – when I got off, patted him and spoke kindly to him. Having led him thro the next gate I mounted again and rode down to Twyford Ferry, crossed the River [Trent] and rode about a mile further, then got off and walked alongside of him and then mounted again. Twice, however, he prepared himself and then it became perfectly evident to me that, if at all startled, the agitation of his nerves not having at all subsided he would do the same thing again. I got off and led him between three and four miles to Ticknall, where I gave him to one of my servants, whom I met with, to take him home and send a Poney for me to ride home upon – and thus, by God's infinite mercy, I arrived safe at home once more. Now I believe I have not often, if ever, been in greater danger than I was at that moment.

December 19th

Yesterday was the first day of the General Election for the county of Derby. The candidates – Vernon – Waterpark – and Greisley. The first rather a radical, the second an honest man, but a strong Whig – the last has been a violent Ultra Tory. The two former will no doubt be returned by a considerable majority. This, as far as the Tories, is entirely their own fault. They split amongst themselves, made a breach, and then tried to patch it up with a candidate unpopular with his own party and altogether intolerable to the opposite one. This 12 months ago I ventured to prophesy would be the case, but they would not credit me – and they now will have to chew the cud of bitter experience. A House divided against itself must fall.

[George John Vernon, eldest son and heir of Lord Vernon, of Sudbury Hall, Derbyshire: Henry Manners Cavendish, 4th Lord Waterpark (an Irish peerage), of Doveridge Hall, Derbyshire: Sir Roger Greisley (now spelt Gresley), of Drakelow Hall, Derbyshire. The election was won by the Whigs].

December 25th, 1832. Christmas Day.

This will not be a merry Christmas to me. My dear wife is from home in the chamber of death. My dear boy John is very ill in bed – and I am not able to attend the Church and the blessed Sacrament which will be administered there this day. God's will be done – may the Lord Jesus sanctify this day to my soul, altho it be spent in the privacy of my own chamber in attendance upon my sick child. Last night I entertained the hope that my dear Boy was much better, but this morning the Fever has returned. He complains of a sore throat and I cannot but apprehend, knowing how much the disease prevails, that it may prove to be Scarlet Fever or Scarlatina.

January 10th, 1833. Harleston, Norfolk.

I commence my remarks this year later than I usually do . . . In consequence of my dear wife's announcement of her poor Father's approaching departure from this world I had determined, so soon as my public business permitted, that I would leave home for Norfolk, my dear wife having prepared a house, which we have borrowed in Harleston, for the reception of myself and the dear children. My dear boy John and I left Calke on the 31st December 1832 – reached Thrapston that night, and arrived in safety at this house on the evening of New Year's Day about 1/2 past 8 o'clock. I don't know that I ever spent a New Year's Day on a journey before. When I arrived I found my dear Father-in-law was gone. He breathed his last on Saturday, the 29th of December 1832 – about 11 o'clock am.

February 1st, 1833

Here is arrived to me the anniversary of my Birth. Thirty eight years has it pleased God, of his wonderful mercy thro Jesus Christ, to preserve me, a poor unworthy sinner, in this world.

February 24th

As I was coming upstairs my dear wife asked me to look into our nursery to see our dear boy, George, who is rather unwell with a feverish cold. As I saw the dear little ones, sleeping in their cots – and could not but gaze with admiration on their cherub faces – so pretty in their sleep – and as I returned to this room, in one corner of which lies our eldest boy in comfortable sleep, I could not but ask myself "Has not the Lord spoken to me in the gift of these dear children?"

March 5th. Harleston.

Yesterday being a beautiful spring day and dry, altho the easterly wind was cold, gave us cause for thankfulness, so great was the relief after 3 weeks of almost incessant rain or snow. I met Mr. Ayton at Billingford to course. I enjoyed my ride exceedingly – we had what would be called a very bad day's sport, finding scarcely any hares and killing but one. Now this suited me – the ride about the field and the sight of those most beautiful of all animals of that species, the "Greyhound", is quite sufficient for me, and the more Hares escape to my mind the better, excepting where they are so numerous as to injure the farmers' crops, and in that case they must be destroyed.

March 17th. Sunday. Calke Abbey.

I left Harleston on Tuesday morning last, slept at Wansford that night and reached this place on the following day about 1/2 past 3 o'clock. I had a cold, but otherwise very pleasant journey. I found this house looking dull, being nearly empty, the country looking very bleak from the prevalence of Easterly winds. On Friday I was very busy all the morning with a variety of occupations such as my agent afforded me. At 2 o'clock I rode to Repton Park to see my brother Charles' new house and afterwards to dine with Caroline and Edmund. They seem very happy, but it is early at present and they are lovers as yet.

March 24th, 1833. Sunday. Huntingdon – George Hotel.

This day finds me thus far upon my return into Suffolk from the Assize at Derby. I left Calke on Tuesday in last week for Breadsall Rectory on a visit to my elder brother. I dined and slept there – and much delighted was I with my visit. it is indeed a most gratifying sight to see him, having escaped the vanities, follies and pollution too common to youth, settled comfortably with his wife and three lovely children, labouring diligently as a minister of the Gospel and sincerely devoted, as he was, in ordination and solemnly dedicated to that holy occupation.

On Wednesday I rode to meet the High Sheriff, Mr. Harrington, of Snelston Hall – dined with him, and then, having accompanied him to meet the Judges in the evening, went to Mr. Simpson's, my solicitor, who was kind enough to give me lodging at his house. On Thursday the Grand Jury were sworn in at 11 o'clock. We sat until past six, then dined with the Judges Denman and

Bosanquet whom we found very attentive and agreeable.

The next day, Friday, we met at $1/2$ past nine and, concluding our business, were dismissed at 6 o'clock. The same evening, I accompanied Mr. Simpson to dine with my excellent friend Mr. Samuel Evans, to meet the High Sheriff, and yesterday morning at $1/2$ past 9 I started from Derby, halted nowhere on the road and reached this place about a $1/4$ past 7 pm. I had intended to proceed to Cambridge, but felt fatigued, and therefore judged it best to remain here.

March 26th. Harleston.

By God's mercy I arrived here in safety about 6 o'clock yesterday evening, finding my dear wife indifferent as well as my eldest boy, but the other three children quite well and merry. I had a safe tho not a pleasant journey, the wind was piercingly cold, and after we turned the angle at Bury St. Edmunds to travel northwards the rain, sleet and snow were incessant in our teeth.

May 13th. Calke Abbey.

I sit down to record a circumstance whose detail, should I omit to note it now, may escape my memory . . .

In the year 1825, about the month of November, I was informed that a young woman of Ticknall, by name "Ensor", had been sent to the House of Correction, she refusing to filiate her Bastard child – that she had previously had a child by William Rollings, baker of Ticknall, and that there could be no doubt but that the 2nd child was his also.

In consequence of her being sent to prison, the disgrace thereof, accompanied by other cruel treatment, she became ill and soon died, leaving 2 children.

William Rollings had confessed that both children were his, and yet he would not allow the poor woman to filiate the 2nd upon him, but it is supposed alarmed her by most dreadful threats. At last one child was filiated upon him, and the other he denied, and the woman having died before the thing could be investigated, he turned away from his former statement and denied being father of the 2nd child.

No one believing his second tale, he was justly reproached by the Parish with his wicked conduct, and it was, I believe, the opinion of all who heard the tale that his cruelty to the young woman Ensor had been the cause of her death as much as if he had murdered her. Will Rollings had worked for me as "Baker" and, thinking it probable that I should hear what was currently reported to his disadvantage on the 26th of November 1825 ... he came to me to justify himself. I well remember the solemn manner in which he protested, and said he was ready to swear the 2nd child was not his, and offered to bring forward 2 witnesses to prove that the girl Ensor was a common prostitute and no better ...

I told him the matter could now never be cleared up before the world – the only evidence being gone – but that I would warn him to remember there was a record of the whole truth which he could not wipe out, and that the day would come when he would meet with the woman Ensor and the children at the bar of Christ's judgement ...

I further said to him, as he was leaving my room, "Well, William, if your own Conscience acquits you, well and good, you will be happy, let the world say what it will of you. But on the other hand, should your conscience tell you that you are guilty you will never have peace in this world" ...

Since then I have heard nothing particularly about the man, except that he was a wild and dissipated character at times. About two years ago, I think it is, he was intending to be married to a young woman of the name of Harrison, a daughter of a publican of that name at Derby. We heard that the wedding day was fixed, then put off, then fixed again, that Rollings was not well, in fact that his mind had shown symptoms of disorder. At last the day was finally fixed, when I believe only the day before Rollings became raving mad with a Brain Fever – and so continued for a long time. During this paroxysm I am told all his ravings were about the girl Ensor – of his strong attachment to her, saying she was *wife*, etc, etc. At length, however, he got better and was married at last.

Since his marriage he has once or twice had partial returns of apparent insanity, but I believe no very serious attack until a few weeks ago when it became evident the old subject again preyed heavily on his mind.

One Sunday he wished to take a walk with his wife, and he would go into the Church-yard. He went straight to the grave of the girl Ensor, where – as they say – he raved madly about her ... he begged of her not to haunt him so – and said she was present to him day and night. To dissipate these thoughts he was persuaded to go to his Father-in-law's house at Derby, and there, the week before last, he was seized with a fit, and died in a few Hours afterwards, and was buried at Ticknall last week. Nine years it pleased God to spare him, and give him time for Repentance. But alas! I fear he received it not in that light.

May 17th

In awful times like the present, could I daily find leisure I might occupy a considerable portion of each successive morning in recording the strange new events which daily take place. In the beginning of this week no slight alarm has been created throughout the Kingdom by an attempt to commence, in earnest, revolutionary proceedings.

Handbills and placards were issued last week by the Political unions of the working classes in London, calling upon the people to meet for the purpose of considering what steps might best be taken preparatory to the establishment of a National convention, through whose instrumentality the people might procure redress for their grievances and the enjoyment of their proper rights and privileges, it being now evident that such blessings were not to be procured by the means of the Established Parliament of their Representatives.

Government immediately issued a proclamation forbidding such meetings, and also made every possible preparation whereby to prevent it taking place.

A number of misguided persons, however, determined to make the attempt [the Clerkenwell Riot]. A large body of police were in readiness; in the struggle of the latter to execute the orders given to them a desperate fight, it appears, took place in which many of the crowd were injured. It is said that the police used a greater violence than was needful, but the contrary is proved from the circumstance of one being stabbed to the heart by a poniard, and three others severely wounded by similar instruments.

By the mercy of God, the police force was successful, dispersed the meeting, and took several of the ringleaders into custody. And we should be further thankful that the papers of yesterday did not communicate any fresh sad intelligence of renewed attempts at Riot.

May 24th, 1833

Here is another boiling day – even the very weather appears to shew the signs of the times. We have now for a month experienced a continuance and an extremity of heat such as I scarce remember to have occurred, without interruption, even in the months of July and August, and such as I never remember in so early a part of the year as the month of May.

The Influenza, [as] the prevailing epidemic is called, has not abated – altho, perhaps, it may have altered in some degree its character. My dear children are now suffering under it, having violent Fever accompanied with Delirium. Our eldest boy, John, has I hope recovered from the attack. Dear baby Evelyn also has, I hope, got over the worst. Poor Isabel is now very ill, and George appears to be sickening with the same complaint.

June 1st

The heat is so intense that I cannot sit any longer in my study. The Western sun makes it very hot in the afternoon and evening. I have been over to Repton Hayes this evening to see my Brother Charles. I am very anxious about him. I can only pray the Lord to direct him and to order for him, as seemeth best to His unerring wisdom.

June 11th

Yesterday afternoon I rode round the Farm with my eldest boy, John. I could not but remark the effects of the long drought. The corn, at this very early period, at least the wheat, is in ear, and the barley beginning to shew the ear. They Hay-crop in some places is so scanty as to appear likely to be hardly worth mowing. The Clover is brown and dead at the top before it has attained its proper heighth. The general appearance was that which would lead a Farmer to tremble at the consequences. As I rode along I could not but mentally discuss, who knows but ere the Harvest comes we may next be dreading too much wet.

Last night there were several symptoms of a change. The smoke of the Lime Kilns and Coal-Pits was in dense clouds, hovering near the surface of the earth … My boy John and myself were sitting on the Balcony when the carriage returned home from Stanton with the ladies. We heard it distinctly in the Melbourne road and the moment they entered the Park gate I could distinguish the footsteps of the Skew-Bald mare so clearly that I could have ventured any wages in challenging her. To-day when I walked out before breakfast the wind was high and strong, the clouds dark and flying fast. About 12 o'clock it began to rain and since that time it has, with a few short intervals, rained heavily.

June 27th

Last week I went, accompanied by my dear Wife … to pay a visit to our kinswoman, Lady Warren at Stapleford, Notts. We went on Thursday – on Friday, having leisure, I borrowed a poney of Lady W. and rode over to Nottingham, to call at the Lunatic Asylum and enquire about W. Pegg [see the

Old Hall, Swarkestone.
Drawn by G. R. Vawser in 1868.

entry for November 30th, 1831]. I found him quite as ill to his mind as ever, but apparently strong in health and very comfortable. Mr. Powell, the director, asked me if I should like to walk round the House; having never in my life entered the walls of so melancholy a place before I felt at first some reluctance, but thinking that altho the sights might be distressing I should perhaps, under God's blessing, receive a useful lesson I agreed to walk round thro the different Wards.

I scarcely know how to describe either the sights which I witnessed or the sensations to which these thoughts gave me. Generally speaking, in the lower Wards the patients were of a class which it was impossible to look at long. Indeed in some instances I thought the moments we paused to look round the room much too long. The Patients that I saw were at the time but few of them violent. Two – one man and one woman – had the straight waistcoat on and the man was confined by a strap to the Bench upon which he sat. Generally speaking they appeared under good control and to acknowledge the authority of the Governor. I was much pleased with his manner, varying of course according to what he knew to be the circumstances of each case. To some he extended his hand and joked and laughed very familiarly with them. In general he was met with cordiality. Once only there appeared to be great reluctance on the part of the patient to recognise acquaintance with him.

It was very singular to observe the various forms which the mania took. There appeared to be almost a graduated scale from perfect brutality to a slight degree of monomania. Of the former there was only one, and that a very striking instance. There was a woman, about the age of 26 or 28, of whom Mr. Powell told me "She had no reasonable propensity whatever. That of her it could only be said that altho bearing the Human Form she was a mere animal. Nothing whatever, he said, could ever induce her to lie down upon a bed. On the floor on a heap of loose straw, arranged or not as the fancy took her, she would lie like an animal".

He spoke to her, and she made a sort of noise in reply, shook hands, or rather permitted him to shake hers, and when he called her to him from the end of the yard where she stood she came to to him. In the same yard with her was the most violent looking person I saw, who altho she made so much noise was not the most dangerous. Her whole employment all day is walking up and down or round the yard, talking all the time, and when she arrives at a wall facing her she stands, and with very violent gestures and horrible yells, holds an angry converse with some imaginary person. She was the only one who remarked or took any notice of me, as a stranger. She addressed me very angrily, and told me she knew who I was. As far as I could collect, she seemed to take me for some person who had injured her.

In the centre Ward of the 2nd class of Females I found a very talkative old lady, who told me she knew my family very well and that I came from Derbyshire, that she knew a neighbour of mine who lived at Melbourne – a Mr. Earp.

In one of the worst Wards, below stairs, appropriated to the men, I saw a poor man – sitting in a corner, incurable as Mr. P. told me, but quite sane on one point. His fancy was that he was dead. We went up to him as he sat on a bench in a corner: "Well, John, how are you?" said Mr. Powell. No answer was given. The question was repeated many times, but no reply. At last Mr. Powell said "Come John, why don't you speak – you know you hear me". When he mumbled out, rather angrily, "I don't hear". "Yes, but you do" said Mr. Powell. "No" said the man "No, no, let me alone. I am dead I tell you".

"Now John", said Mr. Powell, "You are not dead – why, a dead person cannot speak". "I don't speak" was the reply. Then Mr. Powell told me that on one point he was quite sane – to prove which he addressed him "Well John, what shall be done with that money?" "What money?" "Why, the money you and I so often talk about".

"Oh! d—n the money" said the old man. "No John" said Mr. Powell "don't curse the money that is to be of so much use to you and your poor children". "Well then, do what you will with it" (said he) "you know what I wish". "Well, John, and how many children have you?" I think he said two sons and three daughters. "Where do they live? Are they married or single? How many children have they? etc, etc". All which questions he answered, as Mr. P. informed me, quite correct. "Well then, John, how do you wish the money to be divided amongst them? Share and share alike?" "Ay", said he "Just as you think right, Sir, that will do".

July 12th

This being Friday, and market day at Derby, I generally procure more cessation from interruption than upon almost any other day in the week. I have been so employed of late as to have little or no time for writing. Last week I went to Bridlington and Scarboro, to look at those places with a view to taking a house at one of them for the benefits of a little sea-air and bathing to my dear wife. I had a tolerably pleasant journey. But the dust was troublesome and the N.E. wind extremely cold. I passed the Sunday at Scarborough. During my absence from home I had leisure for much meditation and was called to much and serious self-examination, and I suffered much pain and distress of mind from a review of my spiritual state.

July 19th. Scarborough, Yorkshire.

We left home on Wednesday morning last, about 1/2 past 11 o'clock, for this place, our dear children with us in order that the former might have the benefit of a little change of air and Isabel of Sea-water bathing. We passed thro Nottingham, dined at Mansfield, intending to have slept at Doncaster, but when we arrived there we found both inns quite full and were obliged to go forward to Ferrybridge, 15 miles, which place we did not reach until 11 o'clock at night. The poor children were much fatigued but bore it extremely well – and did not appear the worse on the following morning.

We started on Thursday about 1/2 past 9, dined at York, and reached this place about 7 o'clock pm after a very expeditious and a very pleasant journey. This is a beautiful place – I think I should say, upon the whole, the prettiest watering place I have ever yet seen. The town is large, but the part wherein the Lodging Houses are placed is free from its noise and bustle, and The Cliff, from which I now write, is quiet, commanding a beautiful view of the bay.

August 5th

$^1\!/_2$ past 12. I have just been called upon to witness one of the most distressing scenes possible, the only alleviation of which is that the issue has been far less fatal than might have been expected. I came into the Drawing-room to fetch something into my Dressing-room when looking from the window I saw a large Steam-Packet coming in towards the Harbour. Wishing to take this opportunity of using a Telescope, which I had upon trial, I mounted it and looked for a considerable time. I had nearly given up the Glass when observing two Boats which appeared to be making for the Packet I resumed my station at the window.

It appeared to me that the Steam Boat was coming very straight towards the Boats and nearer than was consistent with her safety. I saw the Captain of the Steamer (the James Watt) step on to the paddle-box and look over – when perceiving the Boat so close ahead he immediately made signal to the man at the Helm to put the Vessel round, which he did with all possible alacrity. But the rush of the water drew the Boat rapidly to the ship, she slipping at that moment into the trough of the waves the boat was swamped in an instant, and the next thing I perceived was six or seven dogs' heads appeared above water, and then first one, then a second and then a third head of a man until I counted 7 or 8. I then felt so certain as to the nature of the accident that I could look no longer, but laying down my glass I ran downstairs, took my hat and made all possible speed to the beach, where I found everyone looking on, quite unconscious of what had occurred, with the exception of one person who, like myself, had been looking with a telescope at the Steamer. By degrees, however, the news spread and several boats started for the Vessel. We on shore could not without glasses perceive what was going on – nor hear any tidings until two boats were seen making for the shore.

In the crowd I hastened to the point where they would land. When the first boat touched the shore a young man jumped out – and threw off his jacket – which being given to a bye-stander – he returned wading to meet the boat, only crying out "Send for a doctor". As soon as the boat touched the strand, out of its bow was brought out something wrapped up in a cloke – evidently a body of some person. This was put into a cart and driven slowly off to the receiving house on the Shore. A medical man was there, who jumped into the cart. The crowd was so great that I did not follow them. Next out of the same Boat was carried out a young, hale, strong-looking sailor who, when he set his feet on

In short, I am in great strait and quite at a loss what course is best to take. I would not knowingly run away from, or in any way neglect, my duties as a Christian, as a magistrate, as a country gentleman, which I fear I must do in some degree should I leave Calke. And yet I do not see how it is possible for me to pay all their just due, to keep up my contribution to my various friends, relatives and dependants, and yet occupy my house at Calke.

August 24th. Scarboro.

I have to record another melancholy instance of the uncertainty of human life. About 5 weeks ago the curate of St. Mary's Church was married, on the first or second Sunday after we arrived here. In the afternoon, having attended Divine Service, my dear wife and I walked home behind the gentleman and his bride, and remarked that they were a newly-married couple. About 10 days afterwards she took the Small Pox – and after being, as the medical men hoped, gone on well with it, it suddenly took an unfavourable turn and on Wednesday last she died!!! Under all the circumstances this is a most striking instance of awful warning to all around – in the midst of youth and health and happiness, so suddenly called away, and leaving her Husband at a moment when, of all others, his mind must be most keenly susceptible to the loss.

August 30th. Scarboro.

In the evening my dear wife and I attended a Concert at the Town Hall, given by and for the benefit of Mr. Wilson, the Organist, a very clever and deserving young man, brought up in the School of the Amicable Society . . .

I did not wish to have gone out this week to any such scenes of Gaiety, but last year owing to his having been improvident, or rather profuse in catering for the public amusement, the expenses exceeded the receipts by £2 and it was the wish of all who knew him to support him liberally. The company, I am happy to say, was numerous, the performance very moderate. After the concert was over the benches were removed and the company – at least the junior part – who felt so inclined amused themselves by dancing quadrilles, which they did very good-humouredly to the scraping of the vilest set of performers I ever listened to. About past 12 we returned home – it had then begun to rain in torrents, and the gale, tremendous as it has since proved, was rising in its fury. It was with great difficulty the Ladies could get into their carriages.

Esplanade & South Sands, Scarborough.   Drawn by W. Bevan c. 1845.

August 31st

Well might I say, *tremendous gale*. About 2 o'clock it blew and rained furiously and so has done without interruption until this moment, ¹/₂ past 12 pm.

An awful night it was. About 5 o'clock this morning a poor fishing boat – a coble as they call it here – returning with a load of Herrings, in attempting to make the Harbour was upset close to the Pier Head, and the three hands on board lost. Another boat from Filey, a fishing lugger, is on shore here close to the Pier, a complete Wreck – of the crew of this all were saved, excepting one poor little boy of whom we must hope the Lord has been merciful to his soul . . .

Just as I was writing this the Nurse came downstairs to tell me that another and larger vessel was in sight making towards the shore. I ran upstairs and saw a heavy-laden Brig, with all her sails split to shreds and tatters, labouring and heaving among the waves. Luckily the tide was beginning to turn, and the wind was on shore, so that the Steersman, keeping his head tolerably straight, was enabled to run her ashore, just opposite the Show-rooms.

My first impulse was to run to my Dressing-room, and there on my knees to offer up my most humble prayers and formal supplications . . . When I had done this, putting on my India-rubber cloak and caloshes, and tying a handkerchief round my neck, I started and with some difficulty reached the Strand, the furious blasts of wind threatening to send me heels over head every moment. There an immense crowd had assembled – the apparatus of Captain Manly [life-saving equipment] was brought down – but the Life Boat appeared from the harbour. This was one of the most painfully interesting scenes I ever witnessed.

The Boat was seen resolutely and quietly stealing along the edge of the shore. When she came nearly opposite the wreck she had a fearful struggle with the foaming waves – but, blessed be God, she was successful. She reached the bow of the vessel, and then we saw the men, who had climbed the rigging to escape the dangers of being washed overboard by the waves, descending quietly, one by one, to the Bowsprit and thence dropping into the Boat, as she came near for that purpose. All were saved . . .

In the meantime a Life was very near being lost by the madness or folly of an individual whose intentions might be good but whose efforts could be of no avail. Several persons, thinking I suppose that they might be able to render some assistance, waded into the Sea, which was shallow, and one man supposing that he could wade to the Ship – or not knowing what he was about – proceeded so far that a wave took him off his legs and it was apprehended he must be lost. But he by the mercy of God regained his legs sufficiently to struggle towards the shore, where three or four stout persons rushed in and saved him from a watery grave. He appeared to be a stranger, as no one knew him – and it was said up the beach that he was drunk, or considerably in liquor.

Having rescued all the men, who were safely landed upon the Beach, the Life-Boat returned to the Harbour, and the vessel lies there, in all probability to be knocked to pieces by the flood tide.

4 o'clock pm

About 10 minutes ago two vessels appeared within sight – a cutter or sloop which tried to make the harbour but could not, and is now gone ashore . . . "Manly's apparatus" is gone down. The vessel lies close to the cliff . . .

The other was a Brig, heavily laden – she was at first running for the harbour, but I suppose seeing three vessels wrecked and the one brig . . . upon the beach, she tacked and stood out straight to sea. As far as I could see with my glass she appeared to have all her sail tight and snugly set.

9 o'clock pm

The rain has ceased but the gale at present appears unabated. The crew of the cutter, or sloop – The Perseverance of Scarboro, laden with coal – consisting of two men and a boy, I am thankful to record, were saved by a rope conveyed to them by Capt. Manly's apparatus – altho most awkwardly and clumsily managed. The Poor boy, owing to their bad management, was very nearly drowned in being dragged thro the waves to the shore.

The accounts from Filey are very distressing – six boats were unaccounted for at 12 o'clock to-day. The gale appears to have been so sudden that all were taken by surprise.

September 2nd

Thank God in the course of last night the gale quite subsided and, excepting the agitation which we must expect to continue in the waves for some few days yet, the sea is calm again.

September 3rd

To-day I have been principally engaged in attending to business relative to the effects of the late storm. A meeting of the Gentlemen who are visiting having been called, [it] took place . . . at 12 o'clock this day. It was not very numerous, but respectably attended. A subscription was entered into and upwards of £80 was collected in the room. Since that time more has been received, amounting in the whole to £134-10. When the vicinity and the town have brought forward their contribution I trust a considerable sum will be accumulated for the benefit of the poor sufferers which will in some degree alleviate their present distress.

September 8th. Sunday. Scarborough.

To-day my dear wife, John and I intended to have gone to the Morning Service at the old Church, but the morning was so wet and boisterous that the two former remained at home. I and Mr. Bloxam only went.

We had an alarm during the service which, altho it was the result of no very important cause, might – had it occurred at another time – have been the cause of instant death to the vicar. The large weight of the Church clock fell – the cord which supported it, I suppose, being worn out – and came through the ceiling of the Altar recess, just upon the cushion upon which the Clergyman kneels when at the Altar. Had it occurred during the Communion Service it could scarcely have happened but that the Vicar would have been seriously injured, if not killed . . . The noise was very considerable, and as it happened during the reading of the 2nd Lesson was perhaps more observed. I was sitting in the Vicar's pew with him, and went out to see what had happened. Having observed that there was nothing more to fear, we returned. The Clergyman, who was reading the Prayers, proceeded, and all was quiet.

September 9th. Scarborough.

This is a memorial day with me, being the anniversary of that day on which I entered upon the married state, or as it is rightly termed, when I became a "Benedict". Fourteen years have passed away and I have never had cause for one instant to *repent* of my choice – on the contrary, each succeeding year has united more strongly the chains of our mutual attachment.

September 18th, 1833. York. George Hotel.

Yesterday at about 11 o'clock we took our leave of Scarboro after a most agreeable sojourn there of 9 weeks. I certainly do not think that I have ever before met with any Sea-bathing place which I like so well . . .

To-day, having slept last night at Malton, we sent the children forward to this place, and ourselves, with Mr. Bloxam and our dear John, drove to Castle Howard, the magnificent palace of the Earl of Carlisle. The situation of the house is grand and striking, the well-wooded country, interspersed with abundant variety of hill and dale around it, is very beautiful, but on approaching the house it appeared irregular and straggling, and too many marks of not being kept up in a style of neatness and care which its size and grandeur deserve. If this was observable in the exterior, it was still more so in the interior. The collection of pictures is not large, but there are some very good ones – all of which, with the exception of two or three, are in a wretched condition as to dirt and want of varnish . . .

The two "Gems" for which this collection is noted – viz "The offerings of the wise men of the East to the infant Christ" and "The Three Marys" at the Cross – quite realized my most sanguine expectations. The former is in excellent condition, the latter by no means in such a state as it ought to be. There were some excellent Van Dykes, and a Rubens or two, and a Rembrandt of great value.

September 29th. Sunday. Calke Abbey.

We arrived here, by God's mercy, on Friday in the week before last – all well and much benefitted from our trip to the sea at Scarboro. So various are the demands upon our time, after a long absence from home, that I have found it quite impossible to take up my pen before to-day.

October 2nd. Calke.

I am this day about to enter upon a business of very serious importance, in consequence of the pressure of the time and former irregularities in the keeping of my accounts, etc, etc. I find it necessary to take a careful survey of my affairs in order to remove encumbrances, pay off loans, etc, etc. It will be for me to consider how far it is prudent or even practicable for me to remain in this house. This involves a great variety of questions. As the place of my Birth, and the Head Quarters, as it were, of that Station in life to which it has pleased God to call me, it is my natural and proper place. At the same time, if the living in it involves a greater expense than is prudent, it would be my duty . . . to seek a smaller residence more fitted to my present means . . .

October 19th

Last week I was engaged every day but Friday in attendance upon the Training and Exercise of my Troop of Yeomanry, an occupation most foreign to my taste and inclination but which, in these times, has unhappily become a duty. We were to have been inspected on the Saturday, but no notice having been communicated to us, we had dispersed before the Inspecting Officer arrived. On Monday we were assembled in preparation, but he did not appear.

On the afternoon of that day I accompanied my dear wife upon a visit to Mr. and Mrs. Evans, of Allestree near Derby, where we remained the two following days, I being in attendance upon the Quarter Sessions . . .

We dined at the Bell Inn and in the evening attended the concert to hear the wonderful "Paganini, King of all the Fidlers". I was surprised at his executive fervour but more I cannot say. Doubtless he possessed the capability to perform any music in the most superior style, but his exhibition on this occasion was confined to the display of curious trickery – the result of practice more than taste . . . When I consider the enormous sums of money which this musical juggler has accumulated, especially in England, I feel almost sorry that I ever allowed him to receive one shilling out of my purse. I could not, however, but feel some curiosity to hear a man after whom all the people have been running so eagerly and of whose wonders so much as been both said and printed. We slept at The Bell and returned here to dinner.

I am most thankful to say we found our dear little ones well, and they greeted us with unfeigned joy – all but my dear John who, I am sorry to hear, had not been so diligent with his Tutor as he ought to have been and who, from conscious shame, did not come out to receive us. It grieved me to the heart to be obliged to refrain from those caresses of affection which my heart longed to bestow on this dear child, but I felt that I must shew plainly my disappointment and displeasure.

October 19th. Saturday.

This is always a busy day. My business as a magistrate occupied the chief of the morning. After that was over, poor Mrs. Gilbert Hutchinson came into my office to detail her sorrows to me.

Her unfortunate Husband, the victim of his own imprudence, is now in the Fleet Prison, where he must remain to take the benefit of the Insolvents Act. It appears Earl Ferrers, or rather his advisers, came upon him for the amount of

Penalties and costs, due upon the late suits decided against him. No sooner had he done that than the Landlord seized for Rent. They had sold up every thing, stripped the Farm and House of every article of furniture, leaving them the bare walls and floors and nothing else, and not even permitting them to bring anything into the house for their own use. I went down to Ticknall this afternoon to view the premises and I never saw such a scene of devastation in my life. I have often read and heard of such things, but never before had the pain to witness it. I have written to the Agents of the Landlord and I hope I shall be able to accomplish something for the ultimate support of the family who – however blameable their Father may be – are innocent.

October 28th. Calke.

... Yesterday morning I rose, as usual, well with the exception of a slight Headache. I walked before breakfast in the favourite Chapel walk. Immediately after breakfast I took my Poney and rode to Ticknall early in order that I might visit some sick people ...

Thence I proceeded to Church. I had not been there long before I felt those nervous sensations coming upon me to which I am occasionally subject and which had particularly affected me on the Sunday evening previous when reading to my family. I struggled against it for a long time, indeed until the singing of the first Psalm. Then I began to be alarmed lest I should faint, and went out of Church. When I was in the open air I felt relieved – my dear wife soon followed me, and I thought that if I took a turn or two in the Church-yard I should soon be well again. But I felt the tremulous sensation come over me again, and found I had better go into some house. We went into Mr. Thos. Rose's, where Anne Rose gave me a little Brandy, which I drank, but it did not do me much good. I sat in a Chair in the open air, but did not feel better. At last they assisted me upstairs and I lay down on a bed, where for a while I lay struggling with the fainting fit – for such I suppose it was – until Mr. Sheffield arrived, who gave me a strong dose of lavender drops and Aether. They put a bottle of Hot water to my feet and rubbed my hands.

After a second dose of Lavender and Aether I began to recover, and was able to get into the carriage and come home. I have had medicine and, thank God, am much better, tho still nervous at times.

View in Calke Park.
Drawn by G. R. Vawser in 1868.

November 22nd

Here is a peculiar – very peculiar – feature of my present indisposition and one of which I desire to take particular notice. Whilst I can enter into many of the trifling amusements or innocent occupations of life I am incapacitated for the discharge of those duties in which I am best able to serve the Lord my God, to glorify His name and do good towards my fellow-men. I am not able to read Prayers to my Household or to instruct them upon the evenings of the Sabbath-day. I am not able to visit the sick, to be active in the support of the widow, or the fatherless. I cannot attend to my duties as a magistrate or as a Country-Gentleman. I am at present almost a useless member of society. How comes this? The Lord has been pleased to afflict me – my present Master who is in Heaven, who placed me in the situation of Life in which I am, as his servant, has in effect "suspended me in my office", as the technical phrase would have it. Why?

January 26th, 1834. Sunday.

. . . It is a curious circumstance that only on the Saturday before last Mr. Witt and I were conversing on the state of Ticknall Church and remarking how very much too small it is for the accommodation of the public – not capable of containing 400 when there is a population of 2,000 – and I was asking him whether when the Church-yard is enlarged, which by God's permission I hope will be this spring, it would not be advisable . . . to leave also a space as a site for a new Church, should we be able to build one. Now in the last week it was suddenly discovered that the present Church at Ticknall is in a very insecure state. A builder has been employed to examine it, and he says that it is not in a state fit for the public to enter into it . . .

We have first to be very thankful that the Spire has not fallen upon the roof during the time we were at Divine Service. Secondly, I think I cannot do otherwise than perceive that here is a warning that we should build a better temple to the glory of God, and I feel this warning as most especially applying to myself because I am the principal landed proprietor, and the heaviest expense must fall upon me, and the present state of the Old Church decides me at once what is my duty. I must endeavour, by some retrenchment, to make provision for the re-building of this Church in a plain, neat and commodious style.

February 9th. Walcot House, near Diss, Norfolk. Sunday.

On Thursday last we left our dear home on a visit to my dear wife's relatives in this neighbourhood. Our family is now too large to admit of our being entertained in the houses of any of our friends hereabout. Consequently opportunities . . . very seldom occur of our being able to pay such a visit as the present. It happened that, the old house in which we now find ourselves being vacant, its owner – Mr. Manning, the rector of this place – not wishing to occupy it just at present himself, was so kind as to offer us the use of it for a few weeks, an offer which I deemed it right to accept for my dear Jane's sake, and that of her mother, now far advanced in life.

March 9th. Walcot House.

Ever since my illness in the Autumn my chief difficulty has been in the performance of those duties which belong to me particularly as a Christian. For months after my first indisposition I was unable to read Prayers to my family, and even up to the present day I have never been able to perform my usual duty of Sabbath Evening instruction to my family and household – and I have also, which is extremely painful, great difficulty in attending at Church, particularly during the morning service.

March 23rd, 1834. George Hotel, Huntingdon.

Here I am this year also, having been mercifully spared to journey as I did this time last year to the Assizes, and to halt here upon my return into Suffolk. I left Walcot House on the Thursday before last, in company with Mr. Henry Farr, whom I had requested to be my travelling companion, not wishing to be quite alone. We had a very heavy Assize, the most I can ever remember; the Grand Jury had not finished their labours until 6 o'clock upon the 3rd day.

We had one dreadful case of persons charged with murder by suffocating some miners who were working a neighbouring mine in opposition to them. There were 47 witnesses, and it took us upwards of 11 hours to go thro their evidence.

[This remarkable case involved ten lead miners accused of murdering three rival miners on a site at Ashford, near Bakewell, where two seams of ore met. The defendants admitted burning straw, to which "oil of coal" and sulphur had been added, in order to drive away their rivals. All the accused were eventually accquitted. This was largely because of a conflict of medical evidence as to whether death was due to suffocation – as the prosecution claimed – or injuries to the head resulting from the men's panic to get out of the tunnel].

March 27th. Walcot House.

I returned to this place on Monday the 24th after a safe and expedient journey from Huntingdon that morning. I was rejoiced and very thankful to find myself at home, for I began to suspect that, instead of a mere cold, I had got a touch of the influenza, which I find so prevalent in Derbyshire – nor was I mistaken. I went to bed early, fever came on, and my neuralgic pain ensued, by consequence of which I laid awake nearly the whole of the night. I heard the clock strike 10, 11, 12, 1, 2, 3, 4, 5, and a little before 6 I dropped asleep, and restless in pain I continued to doze for nearly 2 hours. I rose, weary and languid, and was confined to the sofa the whole of the day.

April 2nd. Walcot House.

I take up my Pen to record a most melancholy event, as mentioned in the "Globe Newspaper" of to-day. I copy it verbatim:
    "Coroner's Inquest

Yesterday an inquest was held in the King's Bench Prison by Mr. Le Pipre, the deputy Coroner, and a respectable Jury, on the body of John Mytton, esq, who died there on the preceding Saturday. The deceased inherited considerable Estates in the Counties of Salop and Merioneth, for both of which he served the office of High Sheriff, and some time represented the borough of Shrewsbury in Parliament. His princely munificence and eccentric gaieties obtained him great notoriety in the sporting and gay circles both in England and on the Continent. His failings, which leaned to virtue's side, greatly reduced him, and he has left numerous friends to lament the melancholy fact of his dying in a prison which, contrasted with his former splendour, furnishes striking illustration of the mutability of mundane affairs. Two medical attendants stated that the immediate cause of death was disease of the brain (delirium tremens), caused by the excessive use of spirituous liquor. The deceased was in his 38th year. Verdict: "Natural Death" ..."

I once was in company with this unfortunate gentleman at a Shrewsbury Hunt Ball 17 years ago last January. I saw him in the bloom of manhood and in the prime of his wealth – healthy and strong – accompanied by his beautiful Wife. Hers was a short career and, if reports speak true, anything but a happy one ... I think I have heard that he married again, but I forget who. Fox-hunting, Horse-racing, Cock-fighting, the Bottle, etc, etc, occupied the chief of his time and attention and drove him thro the mad career which terminated his existence, in the early period of 38 years – in a common prison.

May 29th, 1834. Calke.

It has pleased God to restore me to my own dear home, after nearly 3 months absence, the last 3 weeks of which have been spent in the bustle of the metropolis – a bustle by no means congenial to my feelings, and certainly injurious to my spiritual welfare ...

In early life London was positively disgusting to me, my pursuits were attached to a country life, and I could not tolerate the confinement and restraint of the great city – added to which its very atmosphere was injurious to my Health. Now my health of body and mind have both undergone some change and it so happened that I found the residence in town agrees remarkably well with me – and I also found that I could turn my attention to a variety of interesting objects in London, which before had either escaped my notice or were not sufficiently attractive, in competition with other objects preferred by me.

July 1st. Calke.

I have been to-day confined to my couch with a violent attack of neuralgic Spasm which has prevented me from attendance at the Quarter Sessions, also from dining with the Revd. N. P. Johnson, Rector of Aston-upon-Trent, to meet the good Bishop of Lichfield and Coventry . . .

Doubtless all is for the best and it is rather curious that I found it so. In consequence of all the Magistrates, both of the Loughboro and Ashby districts, being from home, my home was beat this morning by – I should think – upwards of fifty Poor Pensioners, who wanted to make their Affidavits in order to preserve the Quarterly Payments of their Pension. Had I been from home these poor fellows, many of them infirm, would have had their walk to no purpose. In pain as I was, I managed at last to satisfy them all. After that an unfortunate young woman, who had been guilty of felony, was brought up in custody of the Police Officer of Ashby-de-la-Zouch, whom I was under the necessity of committing for trial at the next Assizes. Then came a young man, who had been shamefully beaten and ill-treated by his Master – so that I was occupied all day and thank God, altho sometimes in most acute pain, I was able to get thro the whole, so that I could see I was detained at home to be useful to others, especially the poor pensioners.

July 19th. Calke.

We have experienced the longest drought without interruptions which I think I ever recollect. The summer of 1826 was hotter and the face of nature was perhaps more scorched by the intense heat of the sun, but I think the earth was not so dry. During the last winter very little rain fell, and I think I may say for the last six months we have not had one thorough day of soaking rain until yesterday. It began lightly in the morning, and soon increased into a steady rain, heavy and incessant, now and then pouring into torrents for 10 minutes and then slackening to its steady pace, and this has now continued for 24 hours, or thereabouts.

August 1st. Great Malvern – The Lodge.

We arrived here this evening, purposing under God's blessing and by His permission, to sojourn here for five or six weeks, in the hope of benefit to the health of all, but more especially of improvement to mine. I have in the course of the last month had two very severe attacks of neuralgia – it was the wish of my dear wife, and the recommendation of all my friends, that I should leave home for a while in order, if possible, by entire relaxation from business to recruit my strength, having once, 4 years ago, been on a visit at this place and found the air very congenial and knowing the Purity of the water rendered it beneficial in all cases of indigestion and weak stomach, and knowing it to be a quiet place unattended upon by the gay world, I selected Malvern.

August 31st. Cheltenham.

During our residence at Malvern and more especially since the weather changed and we have had torrents of rain, I suffered so severely from my neuralgia that at last I came to the reluctant conclusion that the place was much too damp for me. Consequently we removed to this place under the hope that this change, for 10 days or a fortnight, might serve to renew the strength I had lost in my attacks of severe and frequent pain. Unfortunately the weather remained very wet and I have caught cold, with an inflammatory irritation of the mucous membrane which lines the trachea.

I had recovered nearly from the first symptoms, but the wet of yesterday renewed my irritation and last night my cough was very troublesome. The result of this has been that I have not been able to attend divine service this morning at 11.00 am ... We are inhabiting a nearly new house which, altho it is perfectly dry and well-aired, is not always the most wholesome.

September 10th. Cheltenham.

I wish it had so happened that we had been able to spend our wedding-day at Calke – indeed I have in the last week heartily wished that I had persevered in my first intention and gone straight home from Malvern. I have had several very sharp twinges since my arrival here, and altho the attacks have been of a milder character than those at Malvern, yet I am now persuaded that, unless in the depth of winter, I have little to expect from mere change of air and situation.

September 14th. Calke Abbey. Sunday.

Yesterday evening, by God's mercy, we returned in safety to our own dear home, and this morning I was enabled to attend divine service, with my dear wife and eldest boy, at Calke Chapel.

October 5th. Calke Abbey. Sunday.

This afternoon, after Evening Service, I walked with my dear little Isabel to Bradbury's cottage. I found the poor man in a dreadfully weak state, but thankful as he expressed himself to be free from pain . . . His poor wife appeared, as she naturally would do, extremely low but calm and composed. One thing struck me very forcibly – namely the extreme neatness of her house. Not all the hustle or confusion attendant on severe illness . . . had interfered with the usual household arrangements. Every part of both rooms was as clear as possible, her children as neat as ever, and she herself was nursing her infant of 6 months old – neatly dressed as she would have been on any other Sabbath-day.

October 19th. Calke Abbey. Sunday.

I take up my pen to record and to moralize upon a most awful event which has occurred in the course of the last week and which I, for one, cannot help regarding as one of those shocks which generally precede a great general commotion. On Thursday afternoon, about 5 o'clock, some portion of the House of Lords was discovered to be on fire, and by 2 o'clock am both the House of Lords and the House of Commons were reduced by the raging elements to a heap of blackened, smoking ruins. At present we know nothing, perhaps never shall know, any theory of the real origin of the conflagration . . .

It matters not, perhaps, by what agency this awful visitation was accomplished. A visitation we must consider it, and in these times of trial and of trouble one which is ominous of the existence of threatening danger, the heavy hand of which is gathering over our heads

October 26th

It is now a whole twelve-month since I have been able to read and instruct my household on the evening of the Sabbath-day . . . This has grieved me extremely. It is true my friend Mr. Bloxam generally takes my place. But I feel that I am removed from my office and I feel that it is in consequence of my heavenly Father's anger with me.

October 28th

On this day the new Burial Ground at Ticknall was consecrated by Bishop

(Ryder). The day was fine, the assembled multitude were very orderly and well-behaved, and the ceremony was interesting to a degree which will be remembered for many, many years to come.

November 30th, 1834

On Friday last I attended a meeting at the Bell Inn, Derby, for the purpose of considering what should be done, in case of a General Election, for the support of the Conservative interest in the Southern Division of this County. I was called to the Chair, my sentiments being known relative to a determination on my part never to offer myself. I hailed this circumstance of my being called to the Chair as setting me apart, and presumed, of course, that I should not be asked to come forward.

Very early in the meeting, however, the Revd. Reg. Pole took occasion to remark ... that in his opinion, and that of many others, there was one man – and one man only – who in the present state of things could ensure the representation of the Conservative interest, involving as it did the welfare of everything that was sacred and dear to us ... These sentiments were loudly echoed by the cheers of the meeting. I had not one moment for reflection.

I immediately rose and said ... altho I could pledge myself, from my good feelings towards the cause, I could not be responsible for my Health. If, however, when the time came I was so called upon and told that it rested upon me individually whether the Conservative interest had a representative or not, and if it pleased God to give health and strength, I should feel it my duty to offer to my friends my best services. Loud cheers followed this remark of mine.

December 14th. Calke.

Yesterday I was obliged to accompany my colleagues to the market town of Ashbourne to meet the Electors – and about 1 o'clock I found myself standing on a platform on the front of a shop in the centre of the Market-Place in the presence of, I should think, at least 2,000 people, waiting that I should address them ...

When I got out of the window and stepped upon the narrow platform I felt better than I expected, tho when I cast my eye over the dense multitude before me, my nerves trembled. However, I took courage – and was supported. I was enabled to deliver my humble address without agitation of any kind. The multitude were patient and courteous, and I got thro with less uncomfortable consequence than I had anticipated.

Editor's note

Now seems the right moment to end this volume of extracts from Sir George Crewe's journals. Having been pressed into standing as Conservative candidate for South Derbyshire he was about to undergo a radical change in his way of life. Rather to his surprise Sir George headed the poll: as a Member of Parliament, a role in which he was never comfortable, he had to spend more time than he wished in London. How he responded to these new circumstances might be chronicled, perhaps, in a further volume.

Colin Kitching.

PICTURE CREDITS

Grateful acknowledgement is due to the following for their help and permission in reproducing the illustrations in this book.

Miss Airmyne Harpur–Crewe
(Illustrations on pages 15, 16, 22, 29, 38, 41, 49, 55, 66, 80, 89, 94, 97, 104, 113, 127)

National Trust, Calke Abbey
(Illustrations on pages 3, 8, 32)

North Yorkshire County Library
(Illustration on page 120)

INDEX

ALSO PUBLISHED BY SCARTHIN BOOKS

DERBYSHIRE CHURCHES AND CHAPELS OPEN TO VISITORS

Compiled by Rodney Tomkins, Illustrated by Elisabeth Stoppard, foreword by the Bishop of Derby

Illustrated paperback   128 pages   ISBN 1 900446 02 2

TRANSFORMATION OF A VALLEY: THE DERBYSHIRE DERWENT

By Brian Cooper, photographs by Neville Cooper

Illustrated hardback   328 pages   ISBN 0 907758 17 7

THE HISTORY OF THE DERBYSHIRE GENERAL INFIRMARY 1810–1894

By V.M. Leveaux, foreword by Jeremy Taylor

Illustrated cloth-bound hardback 160 pages   ISBN 1 900446 006

THE DIARIES OF MARIA GYTE OF SHELDON DERBYSHIRE 1913–1920

Edited by Gerald Phizackerley, foreword by His Grace the Duke of Devonshire

Illustrated paperback   332 pages + 16 pages of plates
                                              ISBN 0 907758 96 7

HANGED FOR A SHEEP: CRIME IN BYGONE DERBYSHIRE

By E.G. Power

Illustrated paperback   80 pages   ISBN 0 907758 00 2

HISTORIC ORGANS IN DERBYSHIRE: A SURVEY FOR THE MILLENNIUM

By Rodney Tomkins, foreword by Nicholas Thistlewaite

Illustrated cloth-bound hardback 304 pages   ISBN 0 907758 97 5

THE HOSPITALLER ORDER OF ST. JOHN OF JERUSALEM IN DERBYSHIRE HISTORY

By *Gladwyn Turbutt*

Illustrated cloth-bound hardback 64 pages   ISBN 1 900446 01 4

ST. JOHN'S CHAPEL, BELPER: THE LIFE OF A CHURCH AND A COMMUNITY

By *E.G. Power*

Illustrated paperback   40 pages   ISBN 0 907758 11 8

A STAGE OR TWO BEYOND CHRISTENDOM: A SOCIAL HISTORY OF THE CHURCH OF ENGLAND IN DERBYSHIRE

By *Michael Austen*

350 pages + 24 pages Illustration (some colour)
paperback: ISBN 1 900446 03 0
cloth-bound hardback: ISBN 0 1 900446 04 9

DERBYSHIRE IN THE CIVIL WAR

By *Brian Stone*

Illustrated hardback   157 pages, with notes, bibliography and index
      ISBN 0 907758 58 4

DERBYSHIRE CHILDREN AT HOME 1800–1900

By *E.G. Power*

Illustrated paperback   90 pages   ISBN 1 900446 057

http://www.scarthinbooks.com